WALKING IN
THE NORTH PENNINES

About the Author

Paddy Dillon is a prolific walker and guidebook writer, with over 40 books to his name and contributions to 25 other books. He has written extensively for several outdoor magazines and other publications and has appeared on radio and television.

Paddy has walked extensively around the North Pennines for well over 30 years, exploring the moors and dales throughout the seasons and in all weathers. In this guidebook he describes 50 walking routes, from gentle riverside strolls to strenuous moorland treks. Paddy uses a palmtop computer to write his route descriptions while walking, taking note of useful facilities along the way. His descriptions are therefore precise, having been written at the very point at which the reader uses them.

Paddy is an indefatigable long-distance walker who has walked all of Britain's national trails and several major European trails. He lives on the fringes of the English Lake District and has walked, and written about walking, in every county throughout the British Isles. He has led guided walking holidays and has walked throughout Europe, as well as Nepal, Tibet, and the Rocky Mountains of Canada and the US. Paddy is a member of the Outdoor Writers and Photographers Guild.

Other Cicerone guides written by Paddy include:

Walking in County Durham
The GR5 Trail
The North York Moors
The South West Coast Path
The National Trails
The Great Glen Way
Walking the Galloway Hills
Irish Coastal Walks
The Mountains of Ireland
GR20 – Corsica
Walking on the Isle of Arran

The Cleveland Way and the
  Yorkshire Wolds Way
The Irish Coast to Coast Walk
Walking in Malta
Walking in Madeira
Walking in the Canary Islands
  – West
Walking in the Canary Islands
  – East
Channel Island Walks
Walking in the Isles of Scilly

WALKING IN
THE NORTH PENNINES

by Paddy Dillon

CICERONE

2 POLICE SQUARE, MILNTHORPE, CUMBRIA LA7 7PY
www.cicerone.co.uk

© Paddy Dillon 1991, 2009
Second edition 2009
ISBN 978 1 85284 493 6
First edition 1991
ISBN 978 1 85284 084 6
A catalogue record for this book is available from the British Library.
All photographs by the author unless otherwise stated.

This project includes mapping data licensed from Ordnance Survey® with
the permission of the Controller of Her Majesty's Stationery Office.
© Crown copyright 2009. All rights reserved. Licence number PU100012932.

Photo captions
Section 1: An old railway trackbed on the way back to Howgill (Walk 2)
Section 2: A small dam near Haresceugh (Walk 5)
Section 3: Roman Fell from Scordale (Walk 11)
Section 4: The East Fellside flank of the North Pennines (Walk 15)
Section 5: Gill Beck (Walk 18)
Section 6: An old sheepfold on the edge of Monk's Moor (Walk 23)
Section 7: Outcrops of 'sugar limestone' near Cow Green Reservoir (Walk 28)
Section 8: A ruined farmstead on the slopes of Northgate Fell (Walk 32)
Section 9: Above Waskerley Reservoir (Walk 35)
Section 10: A fine track heading off Lilswood Moor to Devil's Water (Walk 38)
Section 11: Two old chimneys above the Allenmill Flues (Walk 42)
Section 12: The River South Tyne between Garrigill and Alston (Walk 44)
Section 13: The River East Allen flows past an old smelt mill at Slag Hill (Walk 47)
Front cover: A walker on the flanks of Harter Fell above Middleton-in-Teesdale

CONTENTS

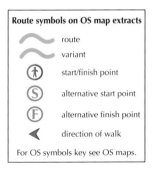

Route symbols on OS map extracts

~ route

~ variant

(†) start/finish point

(S) alternative start point

(F) alternative finish point

◄ direction of walk

For OS symbols key see OS maps.

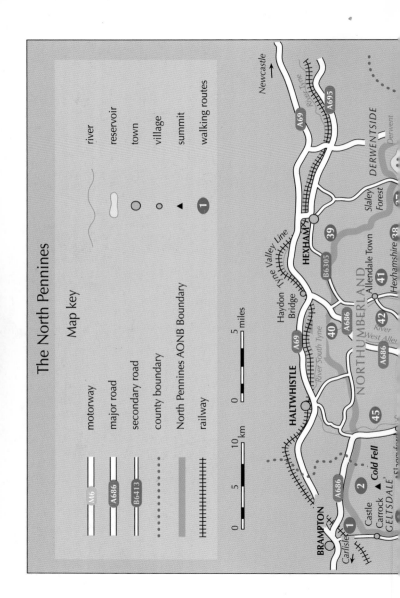

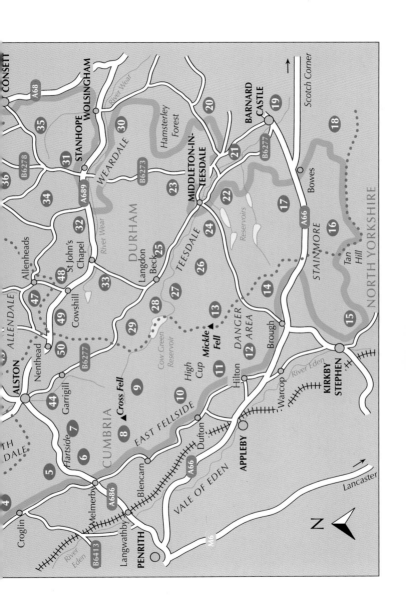

The Whin Sill forms a resistant cliff line around the rim of High Cup on the East Fellside (Walk 10)

INTRODUCTION

The North Pennines has been called 'England's last wilderness', and there is nowhere else in the country where the land is so consistently high, wild, bleak and remote. In fact, this is a region of superlatives – once the world's greatest producer of lead, location of England's most powerful waterfalls, holding several records for extreme weather conditions, home to an assortment of wild flowers, and refuge for most of England's black grouse population. The region is protected as an 'area of outstanding natural beauty', and renowned for its wild and wide-open spaces.

There is plenty of room for everyone to enjoy exploring the North Pennines, with walking routes to suit all abilities, from old, level railway trackbeds to extensive, pathless, tussocky moorland. For many years the region was relatively unknown, being surrounded on all sides by more popular national parks. Since 1965, the Pennine Way has introduced more and more walkers to the region, many of them being surprised at how wild this part of the Pennines is, especially when compared to the gentler, greener Yorkshire Dales.

When national parks were being established in England and Wales, the North Pennines was overlooked. John Dower described a national park as 'an extensive area of beautiful and relatively wild country'. The North Pennines features an extensive area of supremely wild country that isn't matched on the same scale in any of the national parks. The Hobhouse Committee recommended that 12 national parks should be created, and also identified other areas with great landscape value, many of which were subsequently designated as 'areas of outstanding natural beauty', or AONBs. The North Pennines was notably absent from all these listings.

When a document recommending AONB status for the North Pennines was presented to the Secretary of State for the Environment, it was promptly filed and forgotten. A concerted lobby brought it back to the fore and a public enquiry was launched. The North Pennines became a minor battleground, with 'No to AONB' signs appearing in some places, while some landowners declared that their property had no beauty. In June of 1988 the North Pennines was at last declared an area of outstanding natural beauty, becoming the 38th such designation and, at 2000km² (772 square miles), also the largest at that time. This was almost immediately followed by a renewed call for national park status to be granted.

The AONB boundary is roughly enclosed, in a clockwise direction, by Hexham, Consett, Barnard

Castle, Kirkby Stephen, Appleby and Brampton. While all those places lie outside the boundary, each could be considered a 'gateway' to the North Pennines. The largest town inside the AONB is Alston, but Stanhope and Middleton-in-Teesdale are only just outside the boundary.

The AONB includes all the high ground and most of the dales, though half of Teesdale and Weardale are excluded, along with the large forests at Hamsterley and Slaley. Some land south of the busy A66, which was never claimed by the Yorkshire Dales National Park, has been included in the North Pennines. The counties of Cumbria, Durham and Northumberland each claim a third share of the North Pennines, and an office administering the AONB has been established at Stanhope.

The North Pennines was once the world's greatest producer of lead, providing everything from roofing material for churches to lead shot for warfare. A considerable quantity of silver was also mined. The broad, bleak and boggy heather moorlands have long been managed for the sport of grouse shooting, and are best seen when flushed purple in high summer. For many years, walkers wanting to reach the most remote and untrodden parts of the North Pennines might have been put off because of the lack of rights of way, but the recent Countryside and Rights of Way Act 2000 has resulted in vast areas being designated 'access land'.

There has probably never been a better time to explore the North Pennines and this guidebook contains detailed descriptions of 50 one-day walks. These cover nearly 800km (500 miles) of rich and varied terrain, serving to illustrate the region's history, heritage, countryside and natural wonders. This terrain ranges from field paths and old railway tracks to open moorlands on the high Pennines. You will be able to discover the region's geology, natural history and heritage by following informative trails, or taking in specific sites of interest along the way. A network of tourist information centres can help you discover the best places to stay, how to get around and what to see.

GEOLOGY

The geology of the North Pennines can be presented in a fairly simple manner, but can also become extremely complex in some areas. The North Pennines was designated the first 'Geopark' in Britain in 2003, in recognition of how its geology and mineral wealth have shaped the region. The oldest known bedrock is seldom seen at the surface, but is notable along the East Fellside. Ancient Ordovician rock, comprising mudstones and volcanics, features on most of the little hills between the Vale of Eden and the high Pennines, but being heavily faulted, tilted and contorted, is very difficult to understand, even for students of geology. Ordovician rock is about 450

Late-flowering hayfields can be enjoyed in Upper Teesdale and Upper Weardale (Walk 28)

million years old and lies beneath the whole of the North Pennines. There is also a significant granite mass, known as the Weardale Granite, which outcrops nowhere, but was 'proved' at a borehole drilled at Rookhope.

Looking back to the Carboniferous period, 350 million years ago, the whole area was covered by a warm, shallow tropical sea. Countless billions of shelled, soft-bodied creatures lived and died in this sea. Coral reefs grew, and even microscopic organisms sometimes had a type of hard external

or internal structure. Over the aeons, these creatures left their hard shells in heaps on the seabed, and these deposits became the massive grey limestone seen on the fellsides and flanks of the dales today. A dark, durable, fossiliferous limestone outcropping in Weardale is known as Frosterley Marble. Even though it is not a true marble, it polishes well and exhibits remarkable cross sections of fossils.

Even while thick beds of limestone were being laid down, distant mountain ranges, being worn away by storms

13

Frosterley Marble

and vast rivers, brought mud, sand and gravel down into the sea. These murky deposits cut down the light in the water and caused delicate coral reefs and other creatures to die. As more mud and sand were washed into the sea, a vast delta system spread across the region.

At times, shoals of sand and gravel stood above the waterline, and these became colonised by strange, fern-like trees. The level of water in the rivers and sea was in a state of fluctuation, and sometimes the forested delta would be completely flooded, so that plants would be buried under more sand and gravel. The compressed plant material within the beds of sand and mud became thin bands of coal, known as the Coal Measures. This alternating series of sandstones and mudstones, with occasional seams of coal, can be seen all the way across the region. The various hard and soft layers can often be detected where the hill slopes have a vaguely stepped appearance today.

Other geological processes were more violent, resulting in the fracturing and tilting of these ordered sedimentary deposits. The whole series is tilted so that the highest parts of the Pennines are to the west, diminishing in height as they extend east. Far away from the North Pennines, there were violent volcanic episodes, and at one stage a sheet of molten rock was squeezed between existing layers of rock, solidifying as the 'Whin Sill'. Deep-seated heat and pressure brought streams of super-heated, mineral-rich liquids and vapours into cracks and joints in the rocks. These condensed to form veins of mixed minerals, which included lead, silver and copper. Associated minerals are barytes, quartz, fluorspar, calcite, and a host of other compounds. Coal mines and stone quarries are found throughout the North Pennines, and the region was once the world's greatest producer of lead.

Most of the rock seen by visitors around the North Pennines is Carboniferous. Younger rocks are found outside the region, such as the New Red Sandstone in the Vale of Eden, formed in desert conditions, and the soft Magnesian Limestone in the lower parts of County Durham, formed in a rapidly shrinking sea beside the desert. Apart from being lifted to great heights, the only other notable geological occurrence in the North Pennines was during the last ice age, when the whole region was buried beneath a thick ice sheet for about two million years, completely freeing itself from such conditions only 10,000 years ago.

Walkers who wish to delve more deeply into the geology of the North Pennines could equip themselves with specialised geological maps and textbooks, or explore the region in the company of knowledgeable experts. Look out for the annual Northern Rocks events, part of the North Pennines Festival of Geology and Landscape (go to www.northpennines.org.uk for details), held around May and June, which includes guided walks, visits to mines, talks and exhibitions. Also look out for 'Geopark' leaflets describing geological trails and curiosities.

THE WHIN SILL

Many dramatic landforms around the North Pennines and beyond owe their existence to the Whin Sill. This enormous sheet of dolerite was forced into the limestone bedrock under immense pressure in a molten state around 295 million years ago. As the heat dissipated, the limestone in contact with the dolerite baked until its structure altered, forming the peculiar crystalline 'sugar limestone' which breaks down into a soil preferred by many of Teesdale's wild flowers.

While weathering, the Whin Sill proves more resistant than the limestone, forming dramatic cliffs such as Holwick Scars, Cronkley Scar and Falcon Clints. Where the Whin Sill occurs in the bed of the Tees, its abrupt step creates splendid waterfalls such as Low Force, High Force, Bleabeck Force and Cauldron Snout.

The rock has been quarried throughout this part of Teesdale, generally being crushed and used as durable roadstone. It outcrops from time to time along the East Fellside, most notably at High Cup, where it forms impressive cliffs. Outside the North Pennines, the Whin Sill is prominent as a rugged ridge carrying the highest stretches of Hadrian's Wall, and it features regularly as low cliffs along the Northumberland coast, including the Farne Islands.

The River Tees displays some of the finest and most powerful waterfalls in England (Walk 25)

LANDSCAPE

Many visitors are drawn to the North Pennines to enjoy its extensive and apparently endless moorlands, while others are content to explore the gentler green dales. The scenery is remarkably varied, but the sheer scale of the open moorlands is amazing. Almost 30 per cent of England's blanket bog is in the North Pennines. It is worth bearing in mind that the moors are entirely man-managed, grazed by sheep in grassy areas and burnt on a rotation basis to favour the growth of heather as food and shelter for red grouse. Left to nature, without sheep grazing and interference by man, most of the moorlands would revert to scrub woodland, with dense forests filling the dales. Open moorlands are splendid places to walk, with due care and attention – more cautious walkers

may prefer to stay closer to the dales, within reach of habitation.

The dales of the North Pennines are each quite different in character. Teesdale is famous for its powerful waterfalls, while Weardale offers more to those in search of industrial archaeology. Both dales are lush and green, grazed by sheep, with small woodlands and hedgerows providing varied habitats for wildlife. Forty per cent of England's upland hay meadows are located in the upper dales. The northern dales are charming, but sparsely settled, except for South Tynedale, which is dominated by the remarkable little town of Alston, clinging to a steep slope.

The East Fellside flank of the North Pennines is awe-inspiring, where the Vale of Eden gives way to a striking line of conical foothills, while the Pennine massif rises steep and unbroken beyond, maybe with its highest parts lost in the clouds.

There are few forested areas in the North Pennines. Apart from the forests at Hamsterley and Slaley, which actually lie outside the AONB boundary, only small blocks of coniferous forest are found. The last remaining 'wildwoods' are around Allen Banks and Staward Gorge in the north, though there are many pleasant woodlands tucked away in all the dales.

There are no large lakes in the North Pennines, but there are several big reservoirs, constructed to slake the thirst of distant towns, cities and industries. Apart from Cow Green Reservoir in the heart of the North Pennines, there is a reservoir at the head of Weardale, several around Lunedale and Baldersdale in the south, and the Derwent Reservoir and a couple of smaller reservoirs in the east.

It is quite possible to choose routes in the North Pennines that stay exclusively on high moorlands without a break, day after day, but most of the routes in this guide include more variety. The long-distance Pennine Way passes through some of the highest and wildest parts of the region, but also includes visits to villages and has long stretches that stay low down in the dales.

MINING

There are no longer any working mines in the North Pennines, but some of the old lead-mining sites have been preserved. The remains of former industry are best explored around the dale-heads at Killhope,

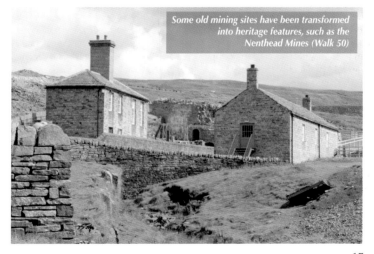

Some old mining sites have been transformed into heritage features, such as the Nenthead Mines (Walk 50)

Allenheads and Nenthead, but there are literally dozens of other interesting sites that are encountered throughout the region. The general rule, when faced with an opening to an old mine, is to keep out. These holes, and the buildings associated with them, are often in a poor state of repair and prone to collapse when disturbed. Only explore in the company of an expert.

Coal mining developed through the centuries in these hills, with bell pits such as those observed near Tan Hill giving way to deeper shafts and levels. Mines in the North Pennines were small compared to the 'super pits' that were later opened to the east in County Durham. Some of the coal had to be used to service the steam engines, including locomotives and static winding engines, working the railways that served some of the larger mining sites.

WEATHER

Some years ago, the North Pennines briefly featured a holiday experience with a difference, called 'Blustery Breaks'. The idea was not to moan about the weather, but to capitalise on it, offering visitors a chance to understand why the North Pennines is associated with extreme weather conditions. It all comes down to the fact that the region is consistently high, with very few breaks that moving air masses can exploit. Put simply, all the wind and weather has to go 'over the top', which results in rapid cooling, leading to condensation, cloud cover, rainfall, and

The North Pennines are broad, bleak, remote and at times subject to wet and windy weather (Walk 8)

in the winter months, bitter cold and snowfall. There is a weather station on top of Great Dun Fell, the highest of its type in England, and naturally this has logged record-breaking conditions.

The broad, bleak moorlands of the North Pennines offer little shelter from extreme weather, so anyone walking in the rain is going to get wet. Anyone walking in mist will find it featureless. Anyone walking in deep snow will find it truly debilitating. It's important to check the weather forecast then dress accordingly. The extensive moorlands are mostly covered in thick blanket bog, great depths of peat that absorb and hold prodigious quantities of water. Sometimes, these stay sodden even during a heatwave. The best time to walk easily across wet blanket bogs is during a hard frost when they are frozen solid!

The Helm Wind

Most visitors to the North Pennines hear about the Helm Wind, but few really understand what it is. The Helm Wind is the only wind in Britain with a name. It only blows from one direction, and gives rise to a peculiar set of conditions. Other winds may blow from all points of the compass, from gentle zephyrs to screaming gales, but the Helm Wind is very strictly defined and cannot be confused with any other. (The last time the author explained how the Helm Wind operated, a film producer from Australia beat a path to his door to make a documentary about it!)

To start with, there needs to be a northeasterly wind blowing, with a minimum speed of 25kph (15mph), which the Beaufort Scale describes as a 'moderate breeze'. This isn't the prevailing wind direction and it tends to occur in the winter and spring. Now, track the air mass as it moves off the North Sea, across low-lying country, as far as the Tyne Gap around Corbridge. The air gets pushed over Hexhamshire Common, crossing moorlands around 300m (1000ft). Next, it crosses the moors above Nenthead, around 600m (2000ft). Later, Cross Fell and its lofty neighbours are reached, almost at a level of 900m (3000ft). There are no low-lying gaps across the North Pennines, so there is nowhere for the air mass to go but over the top.

As the air has been pushed ever-upwards from sea level, it will have cooled considerably. Any moisture it picked up from the sea will condense to form clouds, and these will be most noticeable as they build up above the East Fellside. This feature is known as the Helm Cap, and if there is little moisture present, it will be white, while a greater moisture content will make it seem much darker, resulting in rainfall. Bear in mind at this point that the air mass is not only cooler than, but also denser than, the air mass sitting in the Vale of Eden.

After crossing the highest parts of the North Pennines, the northeasterly wind is cold, dense, and literally runs out of high ground in an instant. The air literally 'falls' down the East Fellside slope, and if it could be seen, it would probably look like a tidal wave. This, and only this, is the Helm Wind. The greater the northeasterly wind speed, the greater the force with which it plummets down the East Fellside, and if it is particularly strong, wet and cold, it is capable of great damage. Very few habitations have ever been built on this slope, and the villages below were generally constructed with their backs to the East Fellside, rarely with doors and windows in them until the advent of modern draught-proofing.

The air mass now does some peculiar things, having dropped, cold and dense, to hit a relatively warm air mass sitting in the Vale of Eden. A 'wave' of air literally rises up and curls back on itself. As warm and cold air mix, there is another phase of condensation inside an aerial vortex, resulting in the formation of a thin, twisting band of cloud that seems to hover mid-air, no matter how hard the wind is blowing at ground level. This peculiar cloud is known as the Helm Bar, and is taken as conclusive proof that the Helm Wind is 'on', as the locals say.

Local people always say that no matter how hard the Helm Wind blows, it can never cross the Eden. All the wind's energy is expended in aerial acrobatics on the East Fellside, where it can roar and rumble for several days, while the Vale of Eden experiences only gentle surface winds. Northeasterly winds are uncommon and short-lived, so after only a few days the system

begins to break down and the usual blustery southwesterly winds are restored. In the meantime, don't refer to any old wind as the 'Helm Wind' until all its characteristics have been noted, including the northeast wind, the Helm Cap and the Helm Bar.

FLOWERS AND WILDLIFE

Although the North Pennines today features extensive moorlands, this was not always the case. From time to time, eroded peat hags reveal the roots of ancient trees – the remnants of the wildwood that once covered all but the most exposed summits. Only hardy species such as juniper or dwarf willow can survive in exposed upland areas, though some of the dales feature mature woodlands, and some marginal areas have been planted with commercial conifers. It may seem strange, but woodland plants can thrive in areas far removed from woodlands, simply by adapting to the shade provided by boulders or other taller plants. One of the best remnants of the original wildwood can be seen around Allen Banks and Staward Gorge, along with the juniper thickets of Upper Teesdale.

Many visitors are delighted to visit Upper Teesdale in spring and early summer, where the peculiar Teesdale Assemblage of plant communities is seen to best effect. Remnant arctic/alpine plants thrive on bleak moorlands – such as cloudberries on the boggiest parts. Drier areas,

◄ *Extensive heather moorlands in the North Pennines are essentially man-managed*

Cloudberries are arctic/alpine remnant plants that thrive on the boggy slopes of Mickle Fell (Walk 13)

◄ *Upper Teesdale boasts a fascinating assemblage of wild plants, including the mountain pansy (Walk 27)*

particularly where the soil is generated by the crumbly 'sugar limestone' on Cronkley Fell and Widdybank Fell, feature an abundance of artic/alpines, including the delightful spring gentian and mountain pansy.

21

Other plants thrive in hay meadows, because haymaking traditionally starts late at Upper Teesdale and Weardale, allowing seeds to mature and drop before mowing. A trip to the Bowlees visitor centre is a fine way to get to grips with the nature and floral tributes of the region before setting off walking and exploring.

Bear in mind that the extensive grass and heather moors of the North Pennines exist only because of human interference. Grassy moorland was developed as rough pasture for sheep grazing, while heather moorland was developed to provide food and shelter for grouse, to maintain a grouse-shooting industry. There should be a greater range of species on the moors, including trees and scrub woodland, but these are suppressed by grazing and rotational burning. Vegetation cover can change markedly when underlying sandstone gives way to limestone.

Most of the animal life you will see around the North Pennines is farm stock, although deer are present in some wooded areas, where they might be observed grazing along the margins of woods and forests at dawn and dusk. Britain's most northerly colony of dormice is found at Allen Banks, and the elusive otter can be spotted, with patience, beside rivers and ponds. Reptiles are seldom seen, but adders, grass snakes and common lizards are present. Amphibians such as frogs are more likely to be seen, while toads and newts are much less common.

Birdlife can be rich and varied, but the North Pennines is notable primarily for their population of red grouse. Rare black grouse can occasionally be spotted, especially during the mating season, when they perform elaborate displays on particular parts of the moors. The place-name 'Cocklake' is derived from 'cock lek', and refers to the mating displays of black grouse. For details see www.blackgrouse.info.

Late spring and early summer are important times for breeding birds. Cuckoos will be heard as they advance northwards, while skylark, lapwing, snipe and curlew are often seen on broad moorlands. Watch out for buzzards, merlins and kestrels in open areas, and red kites around Geltsdale in particular. Herons fish in watercourses, while dippers and grey wagtails will completely submerge themselves in rivers. Some gulls and waders travel from the coast to the Pennines, and it is not unusual to find raucous colonies of gulls around shallow pools high on the moors.

The enormous Upper Teesdale and Moor House national nature reserves often feature guided walks with wildlife experts. Look out for their annual events guide, which runs from March to October, with a special emphasis on the spring and summer. These reserves claim to be the most scientifically studied upland regions in the world! For details, tel 01833 622374 or go to www.naturalengland.org.uk.

Grouse Shooting

Red grouse are hardy, non-migrating birds that thrive on heather moorland. They are deemed to be unique to Britain but may be related to willow grouse across Scandinavia and Russia. These plump birds spend most of their time among the heather, where they are perfectly camouflaged, and many walkers have almost stepped on them before they break noisily from cover, calling 'go-back, go-back, go-back'. They fly close to the ground, with rapid wing-beats, seldom covering any great distance before landing. While young chicks will eat insects, adult birds chew on young heather shoots and various berries.

With so much of the high moorlands used for grouse shooting, it makes sense to be aware of this activity, and to be aware of how the moorlands are managed. The first thing to bear in mind is that extensive heather moorlands are not natural, but have to be created. Heather needs plenty of light and cannot compete with tall vegetation. It can tolerate wet ground, but cannot grow in water-logged bogs. Moorlands may have drainage ditches cut across them to remove excess water, and they may be burnt on a rotation basis, between 1 October and 15 April. When moorland is burnt, heather seeds survive better than other species, and so the plant is quick to recover. However, even the heather itself needs to be burnt, since tall heather has limited food value to grouse, which prefer young heather shoots. Walkers, therefore, will find awkward drainage ditches, deep heather, short heather and scorched terrain. A project called Peatscapes aims to restore some areas of moorland to a natural state, including blocking drains and encouraging species diversification.

Large populations of red grouse will naturally attract predators, including foxes, various rodents and birds of prey, and grouse can also suffer from a debilitating internal parasitic worm. While some predator species are protected, particularly birds of prey, others are not, and are liable to be trapped in an effort to 'control' them. Sometimes, over-zealous gamekeepers have been suspected of killing birds of prey. A particularly sensitive time is spring and early summer, when grouse lay their eggs and raise their chicks, and are vulnerable to attack by predators. Nor do the eggs and chicks fare well if they are constantly disturbed. Dogs should be kept on a leash at this time, and may be banned from some areas of access land.

Once the grouse are thriving in the height of summer, and the heather moorlands turn purple, the grouse-shooting season starts on 12 August. The 'glorious twelfth' sees a lot of activity on the moorlands, with game-keepers leading shooters (or 'guns') from around the world to specially constructed butts, while beaters are employed to drive the grouse towards their doom. Some estates charge a fortune for a day's shoot, and there is still

23

a tradition of getting fresh grouse to the best London restaurants for immediate consumption. When the shooters take a lunch break, they generally retire to a shooting hut. Some of these are rough and ready, while the better examples are often referred to as 'gin palaces'. Grouse shooting is as much a social occasion as it is a sport, and a lot of local people gain employment from it.

Naturally, walkers must expect some grouse moorlands that are designated access land to be closed at various times. There might be a complete ban on dogs, so check in advance whether this is the case (contact the Open Access Contact Centre, tel 0845 1003298, www.countryside-access.gov.uk). Moorlands may be closed during the breeding season, and at times when shooting is taking place. Even if a moorland is open, please tread carefully, as grouse eggs are notoriously difficult to spot. If a moorland is open, yet shooting is taking place, then be prepared to wait courteously for a break in the shooting. The shooting season finishes on 10 December, but towards the end there may be very little shooting actually taking place.

ACCESS TO THE COUNTRYSIDE

Many years ago, when faced with the wide-open moorlands of the North Pennines, some walkers simply assumed that they could walk anywhere, while others were more cautious and concerned about the complete lack of rights of way in some areas. The situation over the past few years has been clarified immensely. Rights of way can be followed by anyone, at any time, but there is also a huge amount of designated access land that can be visited by walkers most of the time. The vast military range, the Warcop Training Area, has not been designated access land, and anyone wanting to walk there will find opportunities very limited.

Large areas of open moorland have been designated access land under the Countryside and Rights of Way (CROW) Act 2000. 'Access land' should not be regarded as offering unlimited access. Some areas are

Prominent signs announce 'access land' and note any restrictions in force

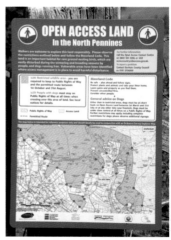

indeed open all the time, but others are 'restricted', and can be closed for various reasons, including grouse shooting and the movement of animals. There may be a complete ban on dogs at any time in some areas, so check in advance whether this is the case. It is always a good idea to check whether any other restrictions or closures are in force – get in touch with the Open Access Contact Centre, tel 0845 1003298, www.countryside access.gov.uk. It is likely that notices will be posted at main access points indicating the nature of any closures. Remember that the access granted is on foot only, and does not extend to bicycles or vehicles, nor does it imply any right to camp on a property.

GETTING TO THE NORTH PENNINES

By Air

Few visitors to the North Pennines arrive by air. Newcastle Airport, tel 0871 8821121, www.newcastleairport.com, has good connections with the rest of Britain, as well as several European cities. The Metro system links the airport with Newcastle Central Station every few minutes for onward travel. Tees Valley Airport, tel 0871 2242426, www.durhamteesvalleyairport.com, is less well connected, but is also a handy option. Sky Express buses connect the airport with the nearby transport hub of Darlington, allowing rapid connections to the eastern parts of the North Pennines. Leeds Bradford International Airport, www.lbia.co.uk, is another option. There are regular Metroconnect buses from the airport to Leeds, enabling a link with the Settle to Carlisle railway line to the Vale of Eden.

By Sea

Ferries reach Newcastle from Amsterdam, bringing the North Pennines within easy reach of the Low Countries. Check ferry schedules with DFDS Seaways, tel 0871 5229955, www.dfdsseaways.co.uk. DFDS runs its own buses between the ferryport and Newcastle Central Station for onward travel.

By Train

Railways almost encircle the North Pennines, but do not penetrate into the area. Cross Country trains provides direct long-distance rail access to Darlington, Durham and Newcastle from Exeter, Bristol, Birmingham, Edinburgh and Glasgow, tel 0844 8110124, www. crosscountrytrains.co.uk. There are also direct National Express East Coast rail services to Darlington, Durham and Newcastle from London Kings Cross and Edinburgh, www.nationalexpresseastcoast.com. Northern Rail, www.northernrail.org, operates along a branch line from Darlington to Bishop Auckland. Carlisle has direct Virgin Trains services from London Euston, www.virgintrains.co.uk. Rail services between Carlisle and Newcastle are operated by Northern Rail, and the same company also runs along the celebrated Settle to Carlisle line through the Vale of Eden, serving Kirkby Stephen, Appleby and Langwathby.

By Bus
National Express runs direct services from London Victoria Coach Station to Newcastle and Carlisle, tel 0871 7818181, www.nationalexpress. com. Some long-distance Arriva buses operate to Newcastle, which is one of the hubs in their network, tel 0870 1201088, www.arrivabus.co.uk. Some long-distance Stagecoach buses operate to Carlisle, one of the hubs in their network, www.stagecoachbus.com. Classic Coaches offers an interesting, regular cross-country service between Blackpool and Newcastle, www.classic-coaches.co.uk.

GETTING AROUND THE NORTH PENNINES

The last time a reasonably comprehensive brochure was produced listing most of the useful bus services around the North Pennines was in 2007. There do not seem to be any plans to reintroduce such a publication, which leaves readers the awkward task of tracking down individual timetable leaflets. This is not easy to do, but essential if you are hoping to use public transport to, from, or around places where it is sparse or irregular. Throughout this guidebook, the names of local operators are given so that contact can be made with

them. The vast majority of routes in this guidebook were researched using local bus services. See also Appendix 3.

By Train
Railways do not penetrate the North Pennines. The Weardale Railway operates only between Wolsingham, Frosterley and Stanhope, but has plans to extend its services in future, www. weardale-railway.org.uk. The South Tyne Railway is a very limited narrow-gauge line running only between Alston and Kirkhaugh, but again there are plans to extend the line, www.strps.org.uk.

By Bus
While some bus operators make their timetables easy to obtain, others don't, and there are several operators running a variety of regular and irregular services around the North Pennines. Bear in mind that very few services run from dale to dale, so there is no real 'network' allowing easy travel from one place to another. You can always walk!

Stagecoach buses, www. stagecoachbus.com, operates regular services between Carlisle and Newcastle, from Carlisle to Brampton and Alston, and from Kendal to Kirkby Stephen. Most of the East Fellside is sparsely served by Fellrunner buses, tel 01768 88232, www.fellrunnerbus. co.uk. However, the villages near Appleby are served by Robinson's buses. Grand Prix buses, tel 017683 41328, www.grandprixservices.co.uk, operate between Penrith, Appleby,

Brough and Kirkby Stephen. Central Coaches serves Bowes from Barnard Castle, while Hodgson's buses serves Greta Bridge from Barnard Castle and Richmond. Arriva buses, tel 0870 1201088, www.arrivabus.co.uk, runs most of the buses in Teesdale. However, the Upper Teesdale bus, tel 01833 640213, serves Upper Teesdale, as its name suggests. Weardale Motor Services, tel 01388 528235, www.weardalemotorservices.co.uk, operates throughout Weardale, as well as linking Weardale with Consett and Blanchland. Go-North East buses, tel 0845 6060260, www.simplygo.com, serves Consett from Newcastle. Tynedale buses, tel 01434 322944, serves Allendale from Hexham and Alston from Haltwhistle. Wright Brothers buses, tel 01434 381200, runs local services around Alston, as well as a very important summer service linking Alston with Newcastle, Hexham, Penrith and Keswick.

Traveline and Taxi Hotline
Timetable information can be checked for any form of public transport in or around the North Pennines by contacting Traveline, tel 0871 2002233, www.traveline.org.uk. If a taxi is required at any point, the National Taxi Hotline can connect you with the nearest taxi service in their scheme, so that you can negotiate a journey and a fare, tel 0800 654321.

Inside Parkhead Station, which is one of the highest cafés in England, above Stanhope (Walks 34 and 35)

TOURIST INFORMATION AND VISITOR CENTRES

In an area as sparsely populated as the North Pennines, where facilities and services are thinly spread, it can be difficult to obtain information about public transport and accommodation in advance. There are smaller tourist information centres ready and able to assist, but the larger ones are only located in the towns surrounding the area. Inside the North Pennines, there are fewer centres, and they may not be open throughout the year.

Visitor centres usually have specialist themes, assisting with the interpretation of the lead-mining industry, transport and other heritage features, or they may simply be general museums illustrating bygone times. Some of them stock basic tourist information, which can be handy if you are some distance from a tourist information centre. See Appendix 4 for contact details.

MAPS

The map extracts in this guidebook are taken from the Ordnance Survey Landranger series at a scale of 1:50,000. Four sheets cover the North Pennines AONB – 86, 87, 91 and 92. One of the routes strays slightly onto sheet 88. While access land is mentioned on many routes in this guidebook, it is not shown on the map extracts. The full scope and extent of access land in the North Pennines is shown clearly on Ordnance Survey Explorer maps at a scale of 1:25,000. Six sheets cover the North Pennines AONB – OL5, OL19, OL31, OL43, 307 and 315. All these maps can be obtained directly from Ordnance Survey, www.ordnancesurvey.co.uk, or from good booksellers, many outdoor stores and some tourist information offices.

EMERGENCIES

Walkers exploring an area as bleak and remote as the North Pennines need to be self-sufficient. When exploring away from towns and villages, take enough food and drink for your needs, along with a little extra, just in case. If venturing across pathless moorlands, especially in poor visibility, ensure that your map-reading skills are good. Pack a small first aid kit to deal with any cuts and grazes that might be sustained along the way. Hopefully, you will not require anything more, but in the event of a serious injury or exhaustion, it may be necessary to call the emergency services.

The mountain rescue, police, ambulance or fire brigade are all alerted by dialling 999 (or the European 112). Be ready to supply full details of the nature of the emergency, so that an appropriate response can be made. Keep in contact with the emergency services in case they require further information or clarification.

The Pennine Way national trail has introduced many walkers to the wildest parts of the North Pennines (Walk 25)

HOW TO USE THIS GUIDEBOOK

This guidebook contains details of 50 walking routes, spread over all parts of the North Pennines. Most are circular, so that anyone using a car can return to it at the end of the walk, but a few are linear and require the use of public transport for completion. Together, these routes stretch nearly 800km (500 miles) across immensely rich and varied countryside, taking in some of the finest and most interesting features of the region.

Read the route descriptions carefully before setting out, and if carrying Ordnance Survey maps in addition to the extracts used in this book, be sure to take the ones listed for each walk. The essential information for each route is given under the following headings.

- **Distance:** given in kilometres and miles.
- **Terrain:** summary of the nature of the terrain and paths used.
- **Start/finish:** usually the same place, but sometimes different.
- **Maps:** OS Landranger and OS Explorer sheet numbers.
- **Refreshments:** summary of pubs and cafés on the route.
- **Transport:** basic bus frequency and destinations.

SECTION 1
GELTSDALE

The extreme northwestern part of the North Pennines is easily reached by way of Brampton and is dominated by the broad moorland dome of Cold Fell. The 'mad' River Gelt drains this area, having its headwaters on boggy moorlands partly protected by the RSPB and partly managed for grouse shooting. The King's Forest of Geltsdale was established in the 14th century and was notable for the hunting of wild boar.

Four walks in this area are described, starting with an easy and attractive low-level circuit in the countryside near Brampton, which is just outside the AONB boundary. Cold Fell is best climbed in good weather and features extensive views, but the ground underfoot is nearly always awkward and boggy. Don't expect to meet many walkers on top. (An elderly local farmer once asked the author to point out Cold Fell, on the grounds that he'd heard of it, but never really

knew where it was!) The King's Forest of Geltsdale is explored using tracks and paths around the flanks of the hills, rather than crossing over them. Croglin Fell, on the other hand, is climbed purely for its own sake. Interestingly, Croglin village achieved some notoriety following a series of 'vampire' attacks in the 19th century.

Public transport to Brampton is good, both by bus and train, but onward transport is quite limited. Some of the little villages may have a bus service on only one or two days in the week. While a full range of services is available at Brampton, facilities in the nearby villages are limited to occasional pubs, some of which provide accommodation. Bear in mind that accommodation in Brampton comes under considerable pressure in the summer months, as it is within easy reach of the popular Hadrian's Wall National Trail.

WALK 1

Brampton, Gelt and Talkin

Distance	15km (9½ miles)
Terrain	Gentle field paths, wooded riverside paths and quiet roads.
Start/finish	Moot Hall, Brampton – 531611
Maps	OS Landranger 86; Explorer 315
Refreshments	Plenty of choice in Brampton. Pub at Talkin. Tea room at Talkin Tarn.
Transport	Regular Arriva and Stagecoach buses, as well as trains, serve Brampton from Carlisle and Newcastle. Stagecoach buses also link Brampton with Alston.

Brampton is a bustling little market town of some character, centred on its octagonal Moot Hall. It is a splendid gateway to the North Pennines. There is immediate access to the 'mad' River Gelt, which rushes through a well-wooded gorge rich in interest and wildlife. The riverside walk links with quiet country roads, later passing the small village of Talkin to reach a popular little country park based around Talkin Tarn. The course of an old horse-drawn railway track, the Dandy Line, leads back to Brampton.

BRAMPTON

A Roman fort lies close to the River Irthing and a small settlement grew up there in the seventh century. It was later cleared as people transferred to a new site, where Brampton is now situated. A Moot Hall has stood in the centre of the bustling market town since 1648, but the current octagonal structure dates from 1817. The area saw plenty of Borders strife, culminating in the arrival of Bonnie Prince Charlie on his white charger. He made Brampton his headquarters in 1745 during the siege of Carlisle. The mayor and aldermen of Carlisle travelled to Brampton to hand over the keys to the city.

Spend time wandering around Brampton, taking in St Martin's Church, Prince Charlie's House, the old stocks, the site of an old bullring, and plenty of fine buildings. Facilities include banks with ATMs, post office, accommodation, plenty of shops, pubs and restaurants. The tourist information centre is in the Moot Hall, tel 01697 73433, open Easter to October, except Sundays.

Follow Front Street away from the centre of **Brampton**, past St Martin's Church, to continue along Carlisle Road.

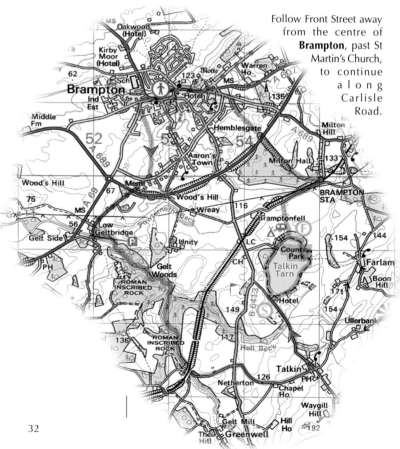

Turn left as signposted for Carlisle along a road called Elmfield. At the top of the road, turn left again through a gate to follow a field path, enjoying views of the northern Lake District and southern Scotland. Cross a road and turn right to follow Capon Tree Road. Big beeches grow beside a couple of houses, then a stone **memorial** marks the spot where the Capon Tree once grew.

CAPON TREE MEMORIAL

Following the retreat of Bonnie Prince Charlie, his local supporters were hung from the branches of the Capon Tree. The tree no longer exists, but is marked by a stone monument planted in 1904. Its name is derived from the capons eaten in its shade by assize judges travelling to Carlisle. They were in the habit of breaking their journey at the tree in order to accept bribes from litigants in advance of court proceedings!

Keep straight ahead to cross the busy **A69** with great care. Pick up the continuation of the Capon Tree Road, following Bonnie Prince Charlie's route towards Carlisle, at least as far as **Low Geltbridge**. Don't cross the bridge, but peer over its parapet to see the **River Gelt** cutting through a dark, red sandstone gorge.

THE 'MAD' RIVER GELT

The River Gelt's name is derived from the Norse 'geilt', meaning 'mad', and is locally known as the 'Mad River', flowing fast, furious and frenzied at times. The red sandstone in this area was quarried by the Romans for use at Hadrian's Wall. With expert guidance you could locate the 'Written Rock of Gelt', where Roman quarrymen carved their names. The varied woodlands support birds such as wood warblers, tree-creepers, pied flycatchers, woodpeckers, song thrushes and blackcaps. Roe deer and red squirrels can be spotted with patience. Mosses, liverworts, fungi and ferns thrive in damp and shaded locations.

A path has been built in the 'mad' River Gelt, leading walkers upstream through the woods

Turn left through a car park to follow a well-wooded path upstream beside the **River Gelt**. Keep right at a path junction to remain close to the river and study its narrow rocky channel. Part of the path has been built in the river, then there are steps leading uphill.

Pass old quarry faces, where the path climbs above the river then descends to cross a bridge over **Hell Beck**. ◀ Climb from the river again, then head downhill and pass some small waterfalls. The path suddenly emerges from the woods to join a road, which is followed straight ahead beneath the towering arches of a railway viaduct.

The little stream of Hell Beck is reputed to have flowed red with blood for three days after a battle in 1570.

MIDDLE GELT VIADUCT

This was one of the earliest skew-arched viaducts in the country, completed in 1853. The masonry is reputed to have been modelled with carved chunks of turnip, so that the stonemasons and engineers could understand how the odd-shaped blocks would support the arch.

Follow the road up through a crossroads and continue to the little village of **Talkin**. The Blacksmiths Arms offers food, drink and accommodation. Turn left in the village to follow another road to the Tarn End Hotel (which may be closed). Turn right along a short path leading to the shore of **Talkin Tarn**, then consider two options.

TALKIN TARN COUNTRY PARK

Legend tells how a village once occupied this site. An angel of God visited, but was ill-treated by all the inhabitants, except for one old widow. In retribution, the village was drowned in the tarn, except for the old widow. Some say that the tarn is bottomless, while others say that on stormy nights the church bells of the drowned village can be heard tolling beneath the water.

Popular Talkin Tarn Country Park is home to the Talkin Tarn Amateur Rowing Club, which was founded in 1859, making it one of the oldest clubs in the country. Regattas have been held here for even longer, since 1849. Facilities for visitors include a ranger service, education cabin, bird observatory, tea room, toilets, campsite, and a path running all the way round the shore.

To continue, either turn left along the shoreline path, passing the boating club, then turn left again as signposted for Brampton Junction, or turn right to walk round the quieter side of the tarn before turning right for Brampton Junction. The latter choice adds very little distance to the day's walk. Leaving **Talkin Tarn**, woods give way to a field path, which in turn leads to the Brampton Fell Road. Turn right and follow the road to **Brampton Station**.

Cross the footbridge over the railway, go through a gate and turn left to follow a track parallel to the railway. The track gradually veers right, away from the railway, and was formerly a railway line itself. The Dandy Line, as it was known, was a horse-drawn line leading to Brampton. It passes woods and runs beneath the busy **A69**, then heads through fields until a missing bridge requires walkers to drop down steps to the right. Turn left along a road and generally keep left to follow roads back into the centre of **Brampton**.

WALK 2
Hallbankgate and Cold Fell

Distance	14.5km (9 miles)
Terrain	Tracks and paths on lower ground, but rugged, boggy moorland on higher ground.
Start/finish	Hallbankgate – 580596
Maps	OS Landranger 86. Explorer OL43
Refreshments	Pub in Hallbankgate.
Transport	Occasional Stagecoach and Wright Brothers buses serve Hallbankgate from Carlisle, Brampton and Alston, daily except Sundays.

Cold Fell is the last big, broad, boggy moorland hump at the northern end of the North Pennines. Cold by name and cold by nature, it can feature snowy slopes long after the nearby plains have thawed. The easiest access is from the village of Hallbankgate, if arriving by bus, while motorists can use an RSPB car park on the road to Howgill.

There is a pleasant grassy path at first, but rugged boggy slopes later. In case of mist, handy post-and-wire fences can be followed across the broad and open higher slopes.

Start at **Hallbankgate**, where facilities are limited to the food, drink and accommodation offered by the Belted Will pub, and the Co-op store. Buses are infrequent, so if relying on them, be sure to check the rather limited timetable. There is an even less frequent bus that runs a little further to a turning space on the road signposted for the RSPB Geltsdale reserve. Continue along this road and pass **Clesketts** to reach the RSPB Geltsdale car park. Motorists parking here can save almost 3km (2 miles) of road-walking from the day's total.

RSPB GELTSDALE

The information office for this reserve is off-route beside Tindale Tarn, but the RSPB has an interest in Cold Fell and much of the surrounding land. Pick up a leaflet from the dispenser at the car park, or if information is required in advance of a visit, tel 016977 46717 or see www.rspb.org.uk. The reserve is centred on Tindale Tarn, which attracts a variety of wading birds, and includes a large organic farm at Stagsike, with flower-rich hay meadows. Nearby Bruthwaite New Wood features a mixed habitat suitable for black grouse. On the higher moors, look out for red grouse, curlew, golden plover and lapwing.

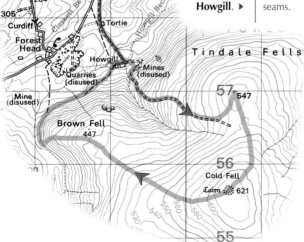

Follow a track straight ahead from the car park, passing a cottage at **Tortie** to approach old colliery cottages at **Howgill**. ▸

Note the little heaps of colliery spoil dotted around this area, marking the position of coal seams.

Turn left through a gate, then right as signposted for the Woodland Trail, and right again for the Bruthwaite Viewpoint. Small areas have been planted with saplings to create diverse habitats for birds.

A grassy path climbs past the Bruthwaite Viewpoint and runs further uphill to cross a stile over a fence. At this point, the path becomes vague, and while the broad slopes of Cold Fell rise to the right, it is actually worth drifting left uphill to reach a tall, columnar cairn on top of a rash of boulders at 547m (1795ft) on **Tindale Fell**.

Face the broad moorland hump of Cold Fell and head towards it, crossing a broad and boggy depression where cloudberry is abundant among the heather and grass. When climbing, drift gradually to the left, partly to avoid messy areas of peat hags and groughs, but also to reach a post-and-wire fence. Turn right to follow the fence uphill and it reaches a junction with another fence. Cross a stile to reach the top of **Cold Fell** at 621m (2037ft).

COLD FELL

A bouldery burial cairn, no doubt the resting place of a chieftain of note, is crowned by a trig point and other stone structures. In very clear weather some of the highest hills in southern Scotland can be discerned, while the Cheviot Hills rise beyond the bristly rug of Keilder Forest. Closer to hand is the Whin Sill, carrying Hadrian's Wall from coast to coast. Criffel lies across the Solway Firth, with Carlisle closer to hand. Looking across the Vale of Eden, the Lake District presents rank after rank of fine fells. Cross Fell, the highest of the North Pennines, lies roughly south.

For the descent, it is best to cross back over the stile then turn left to follow the fence away from the summit. Gradients are gentle and enough people have trodden the rugged moorland to even out some of the tussocks. Keep right when a junction of fences is reached. Later, there is a steep descent on the slopes of **Brown Fell**, where saplings have been planted among the heather.

Turn right at the foot of the slope, following what appears to be an overgrown track. The walking becomes easier later, and the track is actually the remains of an old colliery railway. It is famous for being the last railway that was worked by Stephenson's Rocket. Colliery spoil heaps abound, and eventually a gate gives access to the old colliery cottages back at **Howgill**.

All that remains is to walk back along the access track to the RSPB Geltsdale car park, if you arrived by car, or continue back along the road to **Hallbankgate**, if you arrived by bus.

Old terraced houses at the start of the walk in the little village of Hallbankgate

WALK 3
Castle Carrock and Geltsdale

Distance	22km (13½ miles)
Terrain	Tracks run from valley to valley across moorland slopes, followed by paths and minor roads through low-lying fields.
Start/finish	Castle Carrock – 543553
Maps	OS Landranger 86; Explorers 315 and OL5
Refreshments	Pub in Castle Carrock. Pub off-route in Newbiggin.
Transport	Rare midweek Stagecoach buses link Brampton and Castle Carrock. Rare midweek Fellrunner buses link Penrith and Carlisle with Newbiggin.

Cumrew Fell is almost detached from the main massif of the North Pennines, with the headwaters of the River Gelt draining its eastern slopes, and the little villages of Castle Carrock, Cumrew and Newbiggin lying at the foot of its western slopes.

It is possible to link minor roads, stony and grassy moorland tracks, and an assortment of field paths passing a few farms, to make a complete circuit around the lower slopes of the fell. The first half of the walk passes through the remote King's Forest of Geltsdale, established for the hunting of wild boar in the 14th century, now managed by the RSPB.

The river's name is derived from the Norse 'geilt', meaning 'mad', and is locally known as the Mad River, flowing fast and furious at times through a narrow sandstone gorge.

Start in the pretty village of **Castle Carrock**, where the Weary Sportsman offers food, drink and accommodation, while across the road lies Gelt Hall Farm bed and breakfast. The bus link with Brampton is very infrequent and if used, needs to be checked carefully.

Leave the village by following the Geltsdale road uphill and downhill, continuing straight down a track from **Jockey Shield** to cross an arched stone bridge over the **River Gelt**. ◄

Turn right to follow the track onwards and fork left uphill before reaching a cottage. Keep climbing to pass a gate and later reach a junction of grassy tracks. Turn right here and head gently downhill, enjoying views around the head of Geltsdale.

Pass another gate and follow the track up and down, passing a stout, uninhabited house at **Gairs**, before crossing **How Gill**. The grassy track leads uphill, and the remains of an old colliery can be seen up to the left, before the track levels out at the Gairs Viewpoint at 362m (1188ft).

GAIRS VIEWPOINT

There is a fine view back through Geltsdale from this point, but the sign for the viewpoint actually marks the end of a moorland trail from the RSPB reserve at Tindale Tarn (see Walk 2). Look out for birds of prey, including buzzards, kestrels, peregrines, merlins and hen harriers.

Go through a gate on the heathery slopes of **Tarnmonath Fell** and head downhill, following the track as it winds down to cross a bridge above a small waterfall on **Old Water**. The track climbs again, running as a green ribbon straight ahead, gently up and down on a moorland slope.

An old limekiln is seen on a gap in the moorlands high above the village of Newbiggin

41

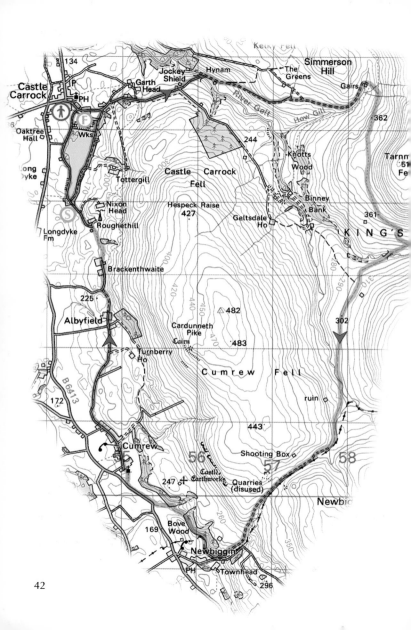

42

The track becomes rather overgrown as it reaches a gate overlooking **New Water**. There used to be a stone bridge here, but it collapsed long ago, leaving only a single abutment. Fording the river will result in wet feet if there has been a lot of recent rain.

A rugged path climbs from the river and gets better further along, becoming a good track. Keep straight ahead at a junction, noting a shooting hut up to the right on the slopes of **Cumrew Fell**. Also look out for ruined limekilns, some distance away on either side of the track, while crossing a broad moorland gap over 360m (1180ft).

The track runs straight downhill, becoming quite steep, and is followed almost to a minor road near Townhead on the outskirts of **Newbiggin**. If a break is needed, the Blue Bell Inn is available in the village.

To continue the walk, don't walk onto the road, but turn right through a gate where a public bridleway signpost indicates Foul Sike. Stay close to a fence beside **Bove Wood** to locate a series of gates leading from field to field.

When a gate leads onto the **B6413**, turn right to follow the road. Keep an eye on a prominent church tower ahead and don't miss the short, but rather overgrown path on the right, which leads through metal kissing gates to St Mary's Church in the village of **Cumrew**.

Walk straight along a minor road through the village, admiring the distinctive roadside gas lamps. Keep straight ahead at a road junction, following a narrower road which later climbs past a small forest.

Don't follow the road to the right, to **Turnberry**, but go straight through gates to follow a patchy road through fields to **Albyfield**. Walk straight past the buildings, through the farmyard, then up into a field and down through another field. When another minor road is reached, turn right to follow it up to **Brackenthwaite**.

Walk straight ahead at the farm then turn right and left, passing through gates as marked from field to field, reaching another minor road below **Roughethill**. Turn left down the road to reach the head of a **reservoir**. ▶

Variant: If time is of the essence, you can stay on the road here and later continue straight along a track, keeping to the west side of the reservoir.

Turn right at the head of the reservoir to follow a track along the east side of the reservoir. When the road is reached, turn left to walk straight back into **Castle Carrock**.

WALK 4
Croglin, Newbiggin and Croglin Fell

Distance	16km (10 miles)
Terrain	Good firm tracks and paths lead onto and off the moors, but there are a couple of river fords and a climb up a rugged moorland slope.
Start/finish	The Robin Hood, Croglin – 574472
Maps	OS Landranger 86; Explorers OL5, OL31, OL43 and 315
Refreshments	Pub in Croglin. Pub off-route in Newbiggin.
Transport	Rare midweek Fellrunner buses link Croglin and Newbiggin with Penrith and Carlisle.

There are no rights of way over Croglin Fell, but plenty of shooting tracks, and the whole fell is designated access land. Apart from a couple of river fords and one rugged moorland slope, most of this route is easy underfoot. The start and finish is at Croglin, but it could easily be restructured to start and finish at nearby Newbiggin. Croglin is a very quiet little village, but in the 19th century it was terrorised by the vampire-like 'Croglin Bat'.

Start at a crossroads in Croglin beside the Robin Hood pub. Follow a road past St John's Church and continue until the tarmac ends. Turn left up a steep and stony track to reach a house. Turn right, then almost immediately left to follow another track uphill and through a gate. Follow a fence straight ahead and turn left at a junction to walk up through another gate.

A broad, walled track rises and falls like a gentle roller coaster as it crosses the hillside, while views stretch across the Vale of Eden to the Lake District, Solway Firth and southern Scotland. Suddenly, the track starts to descend steeply, and if you were to follow it downhill it would lead off-route to the village of **Newbiggin**.

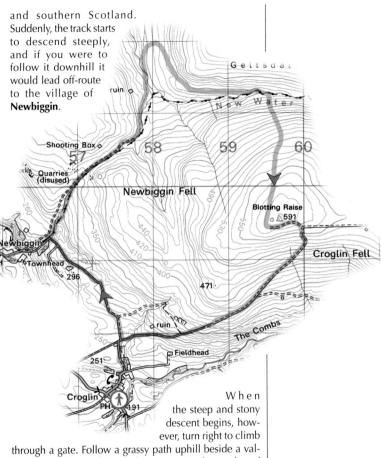

When the steep and stony descent begins, however, turn right to climb through a gate. Follow a grassy path uphill beside a valley, eventually reaching a clear, stony track on a broad moorland gap over 360m (1180ft) near **Cumrew Fell**. There are ruined limekilns some distance away, as well as a shooting hut still further away.

Turn right to follow the track roughly northeast and keep straight ahead down a grassy track. The track narrows

45

and becomes a rather rugged path as it approaches **New Water**. There used to be a stone bridge here, but it collapsed long ago, leaving only a single abutment. Fording the river will result in wet feet if there has been a lot of recent rain.

Climb up from the river and go through a gate, brushing past vegetation to continue along a much clearer track. Watch carefully for a right turn where timbers are embedded in the ground, then follow another grassy track up a slope of grass and heather on the lower slopes of **Middle Top**.

Pass above a sheepfold and continue along the side of a valley, watching carefully to spot a point where a fence crosses **New Water**. Go down to the river and ford it just above a waterfall, caused by an outcrop of the hard doleritic Whin Sill.

There is a gateway in the fence nearby. Go through it and climb up the rugged moorland slope, avoiding deep heather by walking over surprisingly firm areas of moss and rushes. It might be worth drifting left at a higher level to pick up a vehicle track, but this can be rather messy, especially in wet weather, as it has been worn through thick black peat.

The track leads to a stony turning area, where a left turn leads along a track passing through a gap in a wall. There is a trig point just to the left, at 591m (1939ft) on

An outcrop of the Whin Sill causes a waterfall on the course of New Water

the summit of **Croglin Fell**. Views take in the nearby moors, the East Fellside stretching away to Cross Fell, the Lake District beyond the Vale of Eden and Criffel in southern Scotland.

The track snakes invitingly ahead across the broad and bleak moors, but walk only as far as a junction of tracks, and turn right to go down through a gate. A broad and obvious track runs downhill, through a couple more gates, before being enclosed on both sides as it passed above **Fieldhead**.

When a house is reached at a junction, it should be recognised as the one that was passed earlier in the day. Simply turn left, walk down a steep track, turn right at the bottom and follow the road back through **Croglin** to finish.

THE CROGLIN BAT

Twenty years before Bram Stoker unleashed *Dracula* on an unsuspecting world, vampire attacks were taking place at Croglin and were reported in the *Gentleman's Magazine* as chilling fact. In 1875 an Australian family took the tenancy of Croglin Low Hall, where one member, Amelia Cranswell, was attacked in her bedroom. She described a demonic figure, reeking of decay, clad only in a black graveshroud. It burst in through her window, bit her face and neck, and left immediately. A doctor pronounced her injuries to be the work of a beast.

The family packed and took a holiday in Switzerland, but later returned to Croglin and took a number of precautionary measures. By all accounts, the Croglin Bat was at large elsewhere, judging by rumours around the area, but it eventually returned to Croglin Low Hall, where it was pursued and shot. It escaped down into an old crypt, which was later opened by well-armed villagers and found to contain a decomposed body with blood-stained fangs. The Bat's heart was promptly pierced with a stave of rowan, a magical tree, and for good measure the coffin and its contents were burnt.

SECTION 2
THE EAST FELLSIDE

In its fullest extent, the East Fellside is the name given to that formidable flank of the North Pennines that rises from the gentle, agricultural patchwork of the Vale of Eden. The highest Pennine summits rise one after another, with few breaches between them, either for roads, walkers, or even the weather. The nature of the slope gives rise to the peculiar Helm Wind – the only wind in Britain with its own name (see the section on the Helm Wind in the introduction to this guidebook).

Six walks are described in this section, and every one takes in one or two of the red sandstone villages crouching at the foot of the Pennine scarp, and each features the broad and bleak moorland crest above. Take note of the villages, which were all originally tightly built around broad greens, so that crops could be safely guarded and animals herded inside for the winter months, safe from border reivers and other raiders.

Cross Fell dominates the East Fellside, and the Pennine Way National Trail is encountered from time to time on these walks, between Cross Fell and Dufton. Two walks, one along Maiden Way and the other over the Knockergill Pass, run from the East Fellside, across bleak moorlands to South Tynedale (see Section 12).

The Settle to Carlisle railway line runs through the Vale of Eden and allows access to the East Fellside from Appleby and Langwathby, but connections with local bus services are very limited. Fellrunner bus services link some of the villages with Penrith and Carlisle, while Robinson's bus services link some of the villages with Penrith and Appleby. Some East Fellside villages have a small range of facilities, while others offer nothing at all for passing walkers, beyond interesting vernacular architecture and expansive central greens.

WALK 5
Hartside, Black Fell and Renwick

Distance	17.5km (11 miles)
Terrain	High moorlands, boggy in places, with few paths. Walls and fences can be used as guides. Field paths and tracks are used at a lower level.
Start/finish	Hartside Top Café – 646418
Maps	OS Landranger 86; Explorers OL5 AND OL31
Refreshments	Hartside Top Café.
Transport	Wright Brothers buses serves Hartside Top Café from Alston and Penrith in the summer. Rare midweek Fellrunner buses link Renwick with Penrith and Carlisle.

This route starts so high that there is very little climbing onto the moors. Gradients are gentle, and if the weather has been dry, then the ground won't be too boggy. Walls and fences allow easy route-finding along a largely pathless moorland crest, taking in Hartside Height, Black Fell, Watch Hill and Thack Moor. There is an easy descent to the charming little village of Renwick. Payback time comes in the shape of a long walk up a series of old tracks, regaining all the lost height to finish back on top of Hartside. Bear in mind that the Hartside road is one of the first in England to be closed by snow.

If arriving on the summer bus service, start from **Hartside Top Café**, England's highest café at 580m (1903ft). If arriving by car, don't use the café car park, but park in a small limestone quarry round a bend in the direction of Alston. Go through a gate in a fence above the quarry, then follow a fence straight up the moorland crest to reach a junction with a drystone wall at 624m (2047ft) on **Hartside Height**.

Cross a step-stile and turn left to follow the drystone wall across a gentle gap on the moorland crest. The ground is grassy and mossy, while the wall gives way to a fence on a boggy stretch.

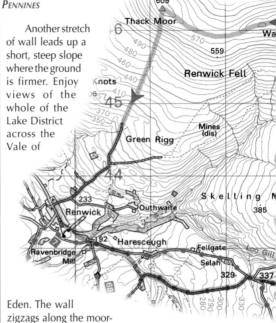

Another stretch of wall leads up a short, steep slope where the ground is firmer. Enjoy views of the whole of the Lake District across the Vale of

Eden. The wall zigzags along the moorland crest, giving way to a fence that zigzags across boggy ground. A junction of fences is reached at a trig point at 664m (2178ft) on **Black Fell**.

The fence running straight ahead leads to Tom Smith's Stone (see Walk 46), so turn left across a step-stile

A ruined sheepfold and shepherd's hut can be seen before climbing Watch Hill

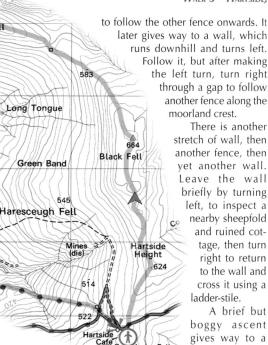

to follow the other fence onwards. It later gives way to a wall, which runs downhill and turns left. Follow it, but after making the left turn, turn right through a gap to follow another fence along the moorland crest.

There is another stretch of wall, then another fence, then yet another wall. Leave the wall briefly by turning left, to inspect a nearby sheepfold and ruined cottage, then turn right to return to the wall and cross it using a ladder-stile.

A brief but boggy ascent gives way to a firmer, pathless slope of grass and moss. Use a ladder-stile to cross a drystone wall at 602m (1975ft) on **Watch Hill**. Head for a nearby grassy hump crowned with a cairn that contains a memorial tablet to someone surnamed Lowthian, dated 1865.

Continue along the broad moorland crest, across a gentle, boggy dip, then cross a step-stile over a fence. Aim for the corner of a drystone wall and keep left of the wall to follow it up to a trig point at 609m (1998ft) on **Thack Moor**. Enjoy views round the nearby moors, spotting Cross Fell beyond Hartside, with the whole of the Lake District stretching beyond the Vale of Eden.

A fence joins the wall beside the trig point, but descend almost due south on a pathless slope, looking

51

along the lower slopes to spot a grassy path that once served a small mine.

A fence and short stretches of wall later lie to the left of the path, leading down to a gate. At the next gate the path is enclosed by walls or fences as it continues downhill. When a road is reached, go straight ahead and down into the village of **Renwick**.

RENWICK

Renwick is a peaceful village of fine, red sandstone buildings. If local lore is to be believed, Renwick suffered the attentions of a 'vampire' similar to that of Croglin (see Walk 4). When the old church was being demolished in 1845, a huge bat flew from the ruins and struck terror into the good folk of Renwick, until it was nailed with a stave from that magical tree, the rowan.

Turn left at All Saints Church to walk through Renwick, but when the road turns right to leave the village, keep straight ahead instead. The road ends at a concrete yard, but a footpath goes through a gate on the right.

Head down through another gate then walk beside a forest to reach a road. Turn left to cross **Raven Bridge** and follow the road straight ahead, as signposted for Haresceugh and Alston.

Before reaching **Haresceugh**, a gate on the right has a signpost indicating two public footpaths. Don't take the one heading straight across a nearby stream, but take the other one, heading up the valley.

Cross a stile from one field to another, then go through gates to keep to the right of a small dam. When a track is reached, turn left to follow it gently uphill. It eventually reaches a road above the farmstead of **Selah**.

Turn right up the road, then take the second track to the left, which is signposted as the C2C and Pennine Cycleway to Hartside. The track is fenced as it climbs, and goes through a couple of gates to pass a ruined house.

A pleasant and grassy stretch leads to a footbridge over a stream, where an old stone bridge is gradually

A white cottage stands beside the road before the final climb to the Hartside Top Café.

crumbling. A path continues uphill, reaching a prominent white cottage just before the main **A686**. Cross the road and climb a short, steep, stony track to finish back at **Hartside Top Café**.

HARTSIDE

The London Lead Company, or 'Quaker Company', managed the most productive lead mines in the world in the early 19th century, but struggled with poor transport links around Alston Moor. The Hartside road needed attention around the same time that John McAdam had settled in Penrith, after writing a book called *The Present State of Road Making*. This was something of a bestseller, and no doubt the Quaker Company was influenced by it. They hired McAdam in 1823 to survey the route and oversee its reconstruction from 1824.

Typical 'McAdamed' roads had sound foundations, lateral drainage ditches, raised surfaces, and most importantly, a surface bound with clay to allow water to run off without taking the road-stone with it. In later years, pitch and coal tar were used to bind the road-stone, giving the world 'tar-McAdamed' roads. (Thank you, Mr McAdam, or should that be 'Ta, Mac'?)

WALK 6
Melmerby and Knapside Hill

Distance	18km (11 miles)
Terrain	A good track gives way to broad and open moorland where careful navigation is required. Clear tracks are used for the descent.
Start/finish	Melmerby – 616374
Maps	OS Landrangers 86 and 91; Explorer OL31
Refreshments	Pub and restaurant at Melmerby. Café at Hartside.
Transport	Rare midweek Fellrunner buses link Melmerby with Penrith and Carlisle. Wright Brothers buses serves Hartside and Melmerby from Hexham, Alston, Penrith and Keswick in the summer.

Melmerby and Gamblesby are charming East Fellside villages. Clear tracks link both places with the high moorland crest of the North Pennines. In clear weather it is a simple matter to stride out along the broad moorland watershed, but in mist this would require careful navigation. The moors are designated access land, but dogs cannot be taken onto the highest parts, to avoid disturbance to ground-nesting birds. In the summer months and on winter weekends, weather permitting, a lunch break can be taken at Hartside Top Café, which is the highest café in England.

Leave the red sandstone village of **Melmerby** as signposted for Ousby. The road bends left to reach Townhead Farmhouse at the edge of the village. Turn left up another road, signposted as a public footpath to Gale Hall and Melmerby Fell.

When the road turns right for **Gale Hall**, keep straight ahead up a track beside a forest. Drop a little to cross a stream, then climb through the forest. The track is flanked by fences as it continues up a moorland slope.

Go through a gate and cross a stream, then follow the track up a slope of bracken beside a drystone wall on **Meikle Awfell**. Note the ancient Ordovician bedrock underfoot.

Go through a gate and follow the track away from the wall, but turn gradually left, up and across a grassy slope to go through another gate in the same wall at a higher level. Climb towards the limestone edge of **Melmerby Low Scar**.

Stay on the clearest track as it winds uphill, passing through one final gate in the wall, close to a sheepfold. The right of way expires here, but all the high ground is access land.

Gently sloping moorland lies ahead, liberally scattered with awkward sandstone boulders. Aim for a prominent cairn, then look directly east to spot another cairn on the horizon.

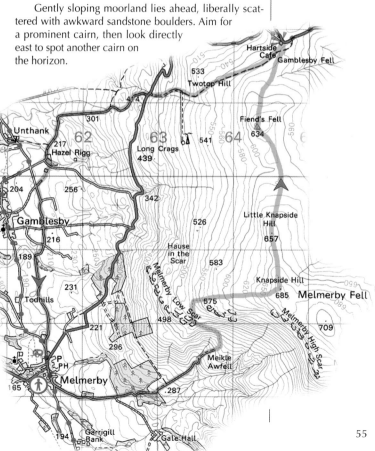

55

*Quiet lanes can be followed from
Renwick back to Melmerby to finish*

Head for the higher cairn and the boulders give way to soggy moorland where a vague path might be spotted. The cairn ahead stands at 685m (2247ft) on the bouldery top of **Knapside Hill**, which is a bump on the shoulder of Melmerby Fell.

Turn left to continue walking northwards along the broad, grassy moorland crest. This is the main watershed of Britain, and is surprisingly firm and dry, though it softens a bit on a broad, shallow depression where a little cloudberry grows. Go through a gate in a fence at 657m (2156ft) on **Little Knapside Hill**.

Make a beeline northwards for the distant hump of Fiend's Fell. There is a vague trodden path lying just off the watershed, crossing squelchy grass and heather moorland.

The path will probably be lost while crossing a little valley, but on the next ascent, head for a sandstone cairn and a path becomes increasingly clear, heading for a gate at the junction of a wall and a fence. Go through the gate and the path leads to a tumbled shelter-cairn and trig point at 634m (2080ft) on **Fiend's Fell**.

Follow wheel marks down a slope of heather and bog cotton, later passing a tall pillar-cairn. (A short-cut is possible at this point, off to the left through a gate in a fence, then down to a stony track.) The wheel marks lead to a gate in a fence, then continue along the moorland crest until a gate in a fence gives access to the **Hartside Top Café** at 580m (1903ft).

HARTSIDE

The main A686 over Hartside is one of the highest roads in England, and one of the first to be closed by snow in the winter. In the summer it carries the highest scheduled bus service in England, operated by Wright Brothers, running between Keswick and Newcastle. Hartside Top Café is very popular with weekend motorcyclists and is the highest café in England. The view outside stretches across the Vale of Eden to the Lake District and includes a glimpse of southern Scotland.

Leave **Hartside Top Café** and go back through the gate in the fence. Follow a grassy track down a limestone slope and note the sudden transition to boggy moorland when the bedrock changes to sandstone.

The track is usually firm and dry, descending gently, then a little steeper through a couple of gates on **Twotop Hill**. Part of the track also serves as an access road to an ugly, girder-work mast, leading down to the main **A686**.

Cross the main road to continue down a grassy track flanked by drystone walls. Later, it is flanked by fences, then one stretch has a line of oak trees alongside. The lower part is flanked by drystone walls again and leads past the farm of **Hazel Rigg** to reach a road junction.

Turn left as indicated by an old sign for Alston, then turn right at a gate with a public footpath signpost. Walk up a small field, then keep left of a larger field, then follow an enclosed track onwards.

When a broad and clear track is reached, there are two options. Keeping straight ahead leads to the lovely red sandstone village of **Gamblesby**, arranged round an extensive green. If this option is taken, then a left turn leads along a road back to Melmerby.

To avoid Gamblesby and the road-walk, turn left along the clear track and simply follow it straight ahead at all junctions. It has some scenic moments and leads straight back to **Melmerby**.

MELMERBY

The village of Melmerby has a broad green and several fine, red sandstone buildings. Facilities include the Village Bakery and Shepherds Inn, both of which have restaurants. Accommodation is limited to Meadow Bank bed and breakfast.

WALK 7
Maiden Way – Kirkland to Alston

Distance	19km (12 miles)
Terrain	Fields give way to open moorland. A ford on the descent can be difficult after heavy rain. Good tracks and roads towards the end.
Start	Kirkland – 645325
Finish	Market Cross, Alston – 718465
Maps	OS Landranger 86, or 87 and 91; Explorer OL31
Refreshments	Plenty of choice at Alston.
Transport	Rare midweek Fellrunner buses link Penrith and Kirkland. Wright Brothers operates a summer bus service between Penrith and Alston.

As the Romans advanced northwards through Britain, they constructed a road across Stainmore and through the Vale of Eden, now largely followed by the busy A66. They also constructed the coast-to-coast fortification of Hadrian's Wall, now followed by a popular national trail. Maiden Way is essentially a link route between Kirkby Thore in the Vale of Eden and the fort of Carvoran, near Hadrian's Wall.

Although some lowland stretches of the old road have been lost, walkers can still enjoy the highest remaining length over the slopes of Melmerby Fell, crossing the high moorland crest between Kirkland and Alston. Maiden Way is one of the highest Roman roads in Britain, second only to the road across High Street in the Lake District. Naturally, this is a linear walk, and leads to the transport hub of Alston.

Start at St Lawrence's church in the tiny village of **Kirkland**. Face the front door of the church, go through a little gate on the left, then pass through a squeeze-stile to leave a corner of the churchyard. Cross a field and cross a step-stile, then walk up through a field.

The right of way actually goes *through* a building standing furthest left at the farm of **Bank Hall**. Turn right

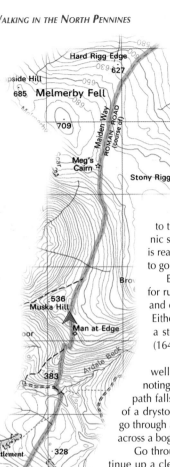

to walk through the farmyard, then left to leave it along a waymarked bridleway.

Go through gates and walk up onto a broad, grassy hill. When a grassy brow is reached, take time to look ahead to spot the continuation of the route. Walk downhill and turn left to cross a wide, flat, wooden bridge over **Ardale Beck**.

Go through a gate in a wall and pick a way up through a steep, grassy valley, with bracken and grass to the right and a slope of crumbling volcanic scree to the left. When a high, grassy gap is reached at the head of this valley, turn right to go through a gate.

Either follow a grassy path uphill, or look for rusting rail tracks half-buried in the grass and climb straight up an old incline instead. Either way, go through a gate to the left of a stone ruin and old mine, around 500m (1640ft) at **Man at Edge**.

Follow a grassy path uphill and keep well to the right of a gap near **Muska Hill**, noting a collapsed limekiln off to the right. The path falls, rises and falls, then passes the corner of a drystone wall. Head gently uphill again, and go through a gate in another wall, then climb gently across a boggy slope.

Go through yet another gate in a wall and continue up a clearer path. Go through a final gate in a wall and climb up a rugged path through a breach on a bouldery slope. **Meg's Cairn** is reached at 660m (2165ft) on the shoulder of **Melmerby Fell**.

Take a last look back across the Vale of Eden to the Lake District. The summit plateau of Cross Fell lies southeast, while the rest of the view stretches across Alston Moor and South Tynedale.

The course of the Maiden Way is indistinct in some parts, but is marked by cairns

MAIDEN WAY

It is possible that the Romans penetrated the North Pennines in search of its mineral riches, but no one knows for sure, nor does anyone know if they had names for their roads. 'Maydengathe' was the name of this route in an abbey record of 1179. Reginald Bainbrigg, of Appleby Grammar School, fed information to William Camden for his book *Britannica*, which was published in 1586. Bainbrigg spoke of 'a street called Mayden Way, which is paved with stones throughout the moors, about some forty miles in length'.

It is anyone's guess how much of the original Roman road has been followed up to this point, but onward progress follows the exact line downhill. The high moorland crest is broad and boulder-strewn, with rugged conditions underfoot.

To distinguish the course of **Maiden Way**, look for a reasonably straight edge of rough masonry and a rather stony surface, with more grass and

map continued on page 62

61

much less heather growing on it than on the surrounding moorland. While some parts of the old road are vague, or have been overwhelmed by bog, there are occasional cairns.

map continued from page 61

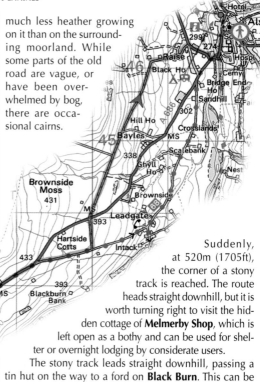

Suddenly, at 520m (1705ft), the corner of a stony track is reached. The route heads straight downhill, but it is worth turning right to visit the hidden cottage of **Melmerby Shop**, which is left open as a bothy and can be used for shelter or overnight lodging by considerate users.

The stony track leads straight downhill, passing a tin hut on the way to a ford on **Black Burn**. This can be an awkward crossing after heavy rain. Go through a gate, follow a track up through another gate and swing left to reach a higher gate. Turn right along a broad, enclosed track to reach the main **A686**. ◄

Variant: If you can arrange to be collected here, or if you can stop a Wright Brothers bus, then the route can be shortened by 7km (4½ miles).

Continue the walk by following the road downhill, which can be busy at weekends, and turn right down a minor road signposted for **Leadgate**. Take the first turning left along a broad track, crossing the **A686** to pick up the track on the other side. The broad, undulating, enclosed old highway is known as the Wardway.

Turn right when a minor road is reached, walking down to a small settlement called **Raise**. Turn right along the A689 and left at a junction by a war memorial to cross the **River South Tyne**. Follow the road into **Alston** and turn right up its steep, cobbled main street to finish in the town centre. (For notes on Alston, see Walk 44, page 213.)

WALK 8
Blencarn, Cross Fell and Kirkland

Distance	17.5 or 22.5km (11 or 14 miles)
Terrain	Good tracks and paths on the lower slopes, but rough and boggy paths at a higher level, some of which are barely trodden on the ground.
Start/finish	Blencarn – 638312
Maps	OS Landranger 91; Explorer OL31
Refreshments	None.
Transport	Rare midweek Fellrunner buses link Blencarn with Penrith and Carlisle.

The majority of walkers climbing Cross Fell follow the Pennine Way, reaching the summit from the shoulders of nearby hills. This route from Blencarn climbs Cross Fell purely for its own sake, savouring its full height and experiencing something of its vastness.

Cross Fell is the highest point in the North Pennines and the highest summit in England outside the Lake District. It used to be called Fiends Fell, recorded as such in 1340 and 1479. William Camden, writing in *Britannica*, published in 1586, said that a cross had been planted on the summit to banish the 'fiends'. It seems they weren't banished far, as there is a Fiends Fell rising northwest, near Hartside.

Start on the broad green in **Blencarn**, following a road in the direction of Milburn. Instead of turning right to leave the village, keep straight ahead on a dead-end road near Cross Keys Farm. A public bridleway signpost at a gate points to Cross Fell.

The first stage of the route exploits a narrow strip of access land flanked by fields. The little farm of **Wythwaite** is passed before the route runs through a gated sheepfold onto the open, lower flanks of Cross Fell. ◄

One can imagine how cattle and sheep grazing these slopes could be herded quickly and effectively into Blencarn without having to pass through any fields.

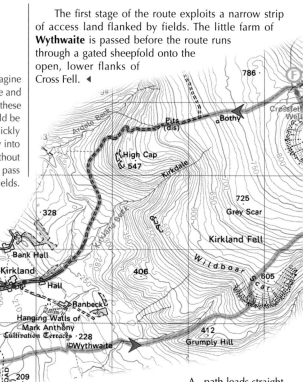

A path leads straight ahead, from grass into extensive bracken, crossing a small stream. Continue following a grassy path through bracken, heading into a valley and across the lower slopes of **Grumply Hill**. Only a little bedrock is exposed, and it is ancient volcanic rock.

The path climbs onto a gap behind the hill, then slices up across a slope beyond, passing limestone on **Wildboar Scar**. The grassy path runs uphill and avoids boulder-strewn slopes, levelling out at a shelter cairn.

Walk up past two more cairns close together, then follow the path up across a grassy slope, littered with sandstone

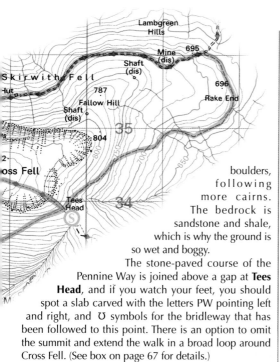

boulders, following more cairns. The bedrock is sandstone and shale, which is why the ground is so wet and boggy.

The stone-paved course of the Pennine Way is joined above a gap at **Tees Head**, and if you watch your feet, you should spot a slab carved with the letters PW pointing left and right, and Ʊ symbols for the bridleway that has been followed to this point. There is an option to omit the summit and extend the walk in a broad loop around Cross Fell. (See box on page 67 for details.)

To stay on the main route, turn left to walk up the stone-paved Pennine Way. The slabs peter out and a tall cairn is passed. In mist, take care to look ahead to spot another big cairn, and beyond that, seek the drystone cross-shelter and trig point on top of **Cross Fell** at 893m (2970ft).

In fine weather there are extensive views, but the broad plateau prevents any sense of depth. The patchwork Vale of Eden stretches to the Yorkshire Dales, Howgill Fells and the serrated skyline of the Lake District. Parts of southern Scotland are in view, and the Cheviot Hills form a conspicuous group. Closer to hand are some of the bleakest and most formidable moorlands of the North Pennines.

The summit plateau hardly bears a trodden path, so head roughly north-northwest and pass a cairn that

Greg's Hut is one of the highest buildings in England, offering shelter on the slopes of Cross Fell

confirms this direction, then drop down a rugged slope at **the Screes** to join another path at a cairn. The remote bothy of **Greg's Hut** can be seen down to the right, but turn left to complete the walk.

The path, known as the Corpse Road, leads over a broad crest on the shoulder of Cross Fell at almost 790m (2590ft), then runs straight down a boggy moorland slope.

The path joins a clearer mining track and continues winding downhill. It is rugged underfoot at first, but gentler once the underlying rock is limestone again near **High Cap**. The track runs down through a gate, then through another gate, crossing **Kirkland Beck** to go through yet another gate.

An enclosed track leads down to a small parking space before Kirkland Hall. Walk along a quiet road to reach St Lawrence's church in **Kirkland**. Keep left at a junction to follow a minor road past a fishing tarn to return to **Blencarn**.

EXTENSION

Taking this extension instead of climbing Cross Fell adds 3km (2 miles) to the day's walk.

When the Pennine Way is reached at **Tees Head**, keep walking straight ahead to go through a gate in a fence. Although this is a public bridleway, there is hardly any sign of a trodden path, so pass a shelter cairn at the foot of a bouldery slope and continue across boggy, grassy moorland, heading roughly northeast. Look across the moors to spot the only track in sight, then head for it.

A couple of marker posts show the way through an old lead-mining site, then the track can be followed with ease, gently up round **Rake End**. The track is remarkable for the amount of purple fluorspar and shiny galena littering its length, and it is tempting to collect a heavy load of souvenirs!

The track follows a drystone wall and goes through gates at a fenced sheepfold to reach a junction with another old mining track above the **Lambgreen Hills**, which is also used by the Pennine Way. Turn left to wind up a boulder-strewn slope, occasionally on bedrock, passing old mines. (Turning right, incidentally, leads down to Garrigill.)

The track continues climbing more gently, passing a ruined sheepfold before reaching the remote bothy of **Greg's Hut**, at 700m (2300ft). This is left open and is available for shelter and overnight lodging for considerate users.

Keep following the path onwards and upwards, reaching a cairn where the main route descends from **Cross Fell**. Simply keep straight ahead for Kirkland along the Corpse Road.

THE CORPSE ROAD

'Corpse roads' are surrounded by a peculiar mythology, but they are simply ordinary hill tracks, used for a variety of purposes, except they were occasionally used to transport the dead for burial. Centuries ago, if one village had a church with a consecrated burial ground, while another lacked a burial ground, bodies had to be packed and carried over the moors like any other goods for shipment. If anyone died in winter and conditions were too harsh for a journey, then they were literally held in 'cold storage' until a thaw. The Corpse Road between Garrigill and Kirkland climbs almost to 790m (2590ft), and is therefore the highest of its kind.

There is a story told of Garrigill folk attempting to take a body over to Kirkland for burial, only to be overtaken by a blizzard and having to abandon the corpse. A further expedition retrieved the corpse, but more bad weather forced a retreat to Garrigill. The bishop was informed of this hardship and Garrigill was granted a consecrated burial ground. Anyone delving into this story will discover inconsistencies, but it serves to illustrate that Cross Fell is wild and remote, and its weather is both severe and fickle. St Lawrence's church at Kirkland has been restored and contains little of antiquity, which is a pity, as its list of rectors stretches back to 1163.

WALK 9
Knockergill Pass – Knock to Garrigill

Distance	12 or 22km (7½ or 13½ miles)
Terrain	A good track and vague path on the ascent, with a road on the highest part. Good tracks and vague paths for the descent, mostly beside rivers.
Start	Knock – 680270, or the Fell Road – 715309
Finish	Dorthgill – 758380, or Garrigill – 745416
Maps	OS Landrangers 86, or 87 and 91; Explorers OL19 and OL31
Refreshments	Pub at Garrigill.
Transport	Occasional Robinson's bus service to Knock from Appleby. Occasional Wright Brothers bus service from Garrigill to Alston.

The Knockergill pass derives its name from 'Knock Ore Gill', which is the stream between Great Dun Fell and Knock Fell. Scottish drovers once crossed the high moorland crest, but whatever paths they used were replaced by mining tracks. These were partly replaced in turn by a tarmac road serving a radar station on Great Dun Fell, and a road serving the Moor House National Nature Reserve. This route allows walkers to pass through the immense Moor House National Nature Reserve, which claims to be the most scientifically studied upland region in the world!

The short form of this route requires someone to drive you high up the Fell Road from Knock towards Great Dun Fell, collecting you from Dorthgill on the Tynehead Fell road later. While you walk 12km (7½ miles), your chauffeur must drive nearly 50km (30 miles) to collect you. Walkers can use footpaths to avoid almost every road while covering the full distance between Knock and Garrigill.

Start in the little village of **Knock** by following the road towards Dufton. When it turns right to leave the village, turn left instead along a farm track signposted as a public footpath. The track is plain and obvious, enclosed as it passes fields.

When a fork is reached, keep right to reach a signpost, then climb straight uphill as the track narrows and becomes a little overgrown. Pass a gate to enter an open field, then drift right, but keep climbing to reach a gate and stile. A grassy ribbon of a path crosses the steep bracken slopes of **Knock Pike**.

Keep looking ahead to line up a series of gates and stiles, well to the left of **Sink Beck**. Keep an eye on Great

A narrow, walled track is followed from the village of Knock towards the slopes of Knock Pike.

Dun Fell and its prominent white radome. There are places where the path is vague, especially on the higher, rushy slopes.

After crossing a final ladder-stile, climb a slope with a large fenced enclosure to the right, containing tree saplings, and a small fenced enclosure to the left, containing weather monitors.

A road appears quite suddenly, flanked with tall, numbered poles so that it can be followed even in deep snow. Climb up the road and it runs close to **Knock Ore Gill** on a slope of sandstone boulder scree.

A junction is reached around 680m (2230ft), where anyone arriving by car for the alternative start can be dropped off. The road runs up through a limestone valley and swings left above a boggy gap between Knock Fell and **Great Dun Fell**. The Pennine Way follows the road from the gap until a gateway is reached at 755m (2477ft).

GREAT DUN FELL

Great Dun Fell rises to 848m (2782ft) and is crowned with a big white radome. The National Air Traffic Services monitors aircraft as well as the weather. Among decades of weather archives lie some all-England records for weather stations, including the greatest number of foggy days, the highest wind speed and most prolonged frost. Bear in mind that the annual mean temperature is only 4°C, while over 200 days may feature mist, and over 100 days feature gale-force winds! The road to the radome is the highest road in England, while the Pennine Way runs roughly parallel up the hillside.

Note the deep 'hush', or gully, on the slopes of Dun Fell, caused by damming and releasing water to scour the hillside and reveal deposits of ore.

Turn right through the gate, leaving the fell road to follow a rugged mining track gently downhill into a huge boggy region with no sign of habitation. The track leads down to an area of spoil that still contains a significant amount of lead ore, or galena. ◄

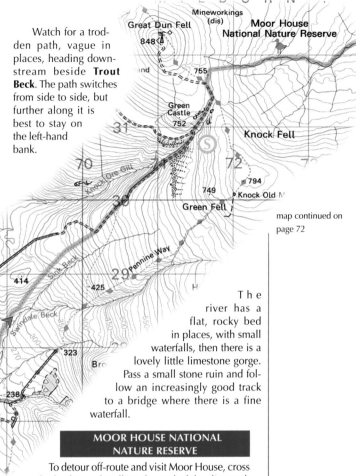

Watch for a trodden path, vague in places, heading downstream beside **Trout Beck**. The path switches from side to side, but further along it is best to stay on the left-hand bank.

map continued on page 72

The river has a flat, rocky bed in places, with small waterfalls, then there is a lovely little limestone gorge. Pass a small stone ruin and follow an increasingly good track to a bridge where there is a fine waterfall.

MOOR HOUSE NATIONAL NATURE RESERVE

To detour off-route and visit Moor House, cross the bridge and walk to the end of the dirt road. The original shooting lodge has been demolished and replaced with a much smaller building. There are no visitor facilities, except for an emergency telephone. In early summer there are interesting wild flowers beside the approach road, such as mountain pansies. (Please do not interfere with any monitoring equipment dotted around the moorlands.)

Follow the dirt road downstream from the bridge and cross another bridge over the **River Tees**, leaving the nature reserve among old mine workings. Turn left along the dirt road, passing a gate, then climb gently along a stretch of tarmac, which gives way to a rough surface again.

There are views of Cross Fell and the highest North Pennine summits as the road passes a shed to reach a broad gap above 550m (1805ft) at **Tyne Head**. The infant River South Tyne has its source just behind a stone sculpture, and at this point the way forward traces the waymarked South Tyne Trail.

Walk gently down the road and note how the river alongside increases its flow. The road climbs a little to pass a dolerite dyke, then drops again and crosses two bridges to reach a barn. ◄

Variant: At this point, if time is pressing and a swift end is needed, follow the road directly to Garrigill.

The South Tyne Trail leaves the road here and continues behind the barn to link various paths together and run roughly parallel to the river.

Follow the marker posts exactly, keeping well above the **River South Tyne** at first, passing little

map continued from page 71

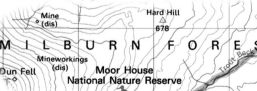

waterfalls tumbling over an outcrop of the Whin Sill. Below the waterfalls is the mineral-rich Great Sulphur Vein, or 'backbone of the Earth', exploited at Sir John's Mine.

Cross a footbridge over a stream below **Tynehead**, and later keep to the right of **Hole House** and its big barn. The river bed features flat slabs and little waterfalls, then an awkward stretch gives way to a grassy track leading away from the river, climbing towards a farmhouse, but keeping well below it.

Cross **Ash Gill** and maybe consider a detour upstream to visit Ashgill Force, otherwise head back down to the **River South Tyne** and follow it onwards. It runs through a dark, wooded gorge, passing one bridge to reach another. Cross the second bridge, which is an old stone arch, and walk up to a road at **Crossgill**. Turn right to follow the road to the village of **Garrigill**.

GARRIGILL

The George and Dragon Inn and a post office shop look onto a fine green, as do a small number of bed and breakfasts. An informal campsite is available behind the village hall and toilets. St John's Hall offers a pool and sauna, for those wishing to relax completely after the day's walk. To continue along the South Tyne Trail to Alston, which runs in common with the Pennine Way, see Walk 44.

WALK 10

Dufton, Great Rundale and High Cup

Distance	16km (10 miles)
Terrain	Good tracks from farmland to the high moors, then rugged moorland walking, ending with a good path and track.
Start/finish	Dufton – 689250
Maps	OS Landranger 91; Explorer OL19
Refreshments	Pub and tearoom in Dufton.
Transport	Occasional Robinson's buses link Dufton with Appleby and Penrith.

Most walkers discover High Cup either via the Pennine Way, or by following a there-and-back walk from Dufton. This walk takes advantage of an old lead-mining track, extended for grouse shooting, climbing through Great Rundale onto access land on High Scald Fell. Although the moors are bleak and remote, the headwaters of Maize Beck offer a sure guide, and the ground alongside has been trodden by grouse shooters.

Maize Beck is crossed by the Pennine Way, which runs along the rim of High Cup. There is no other valley like this in the North Pennines. The sheer, colonnaded cliffs on either side are formed by the Whin Sill – a resistant layer of igneous rock sandwiched between limestone layers – and this is one of its finest moments.

Start on the splendid green in the middle of **Dufton** and walk out of the village as if heading straight for Appleby. The road turns left to pass **Dufton Hall**, but when it turns right, leave it to follow a track straight ahead instead, signposted as the Pennine Way.

At the bottom of this track the Pennine Way heads left, so keep straight ahead and cross a couple of small becks. The track climbs past Pusgill House and is enclosed on both sides until it reaches a gate on the lower slopes of **Dufton Pike**.

If the shapely cone of **Dufton Pike** is to be included as an 'extra', then watch for a path climbing steeply from a gate in a wall on the left. Once the summit is gained at 481m (1578ft), head east for a steep descent to a gate to regain the track.

An attractive water pump was installed on Dufton's green by the London Lead Company

To avoid Dufton Pike, just stay on the track and follow it up through another gate to pass through a gap behind the hill.

The track climbs gently across the grassy flanks of **Great Rundale**, then after passing through another gate it passes limestone outcrops on a steeper slope. Turn round for distant views of the Lakeland Fells, then pass a lime-kiln and cross **Great Rundale Beck**.

The track bends as it climbs, then stays close to the valley floor, passing bare areas of mining spoil where minerals such as calcite and barytes can be gathered. At a higher level the track passes sandstone boulder scree, as well as one last little hump of mining spoil. The track levels out on peaty heather moorland, reaching a **stone hut** around 680m (2230ft) that offers basic shelter from the weather.

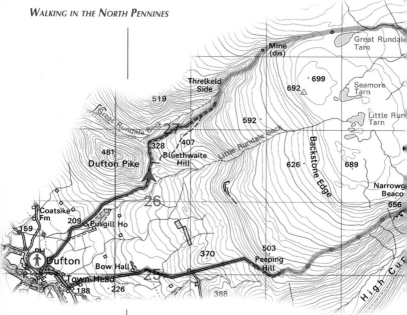

Step up from the track to see
Great Rundale Tarn nearby, then head for its outflow. The heather moorland also supports bog cotton,
crowberry and cloudberry.

Usually, the easiest walking is found to the left-hand
side of the stream, but feel free to switch from side to
side on the way downstream. Sometimes the streambed
is bare rock, but mostly it is a jumble of stones with tiny
waterfalls over rock-steps. Later, it is best to keep to the
right-hand side of **Maize Beck**, before it is funnelled into
a limestone ravine.

◄ Head roughly south to gain the best possible
views from **High Cup Nick** – a bouldery rift at the head
of the awesome **High Cup** valley. In clear weather the
fells of the Lake District are framed beyond the valley
mouth.

Turn right to walk along the top of the cliffs – this
is one of the best parts of the Pennine Way. There is a

Variant: The Pennine
Way crosses a
footbridge over
Maize Beck, then
heads roughly
southwest across
High Cup Plain.

glimpse down to a slender column of rock called Nichol's Chair. ▶

The path becomes narrow and rocky at appropriately named **Narrowgate**, and also passes a couple of gushing springs. The path climbs alongside the valley rim before descending to a gated sheepfold at **Peeping Hill**.

A clear track runs downhill, with Dufton Pike prominent ahead, then the track swings left to go through a gate, heading more directly for Dufton. Go through another gate and the track is enclosed, then, after passing yet another gate, it becomes a narrow tarmac road. Drop down past **Bow Hall** to reach a road junction at **Town Head**, then turn right to follow the road into **Dufton** to finish.

According to a local story, Nichol was a Dufton cobbler who scaled the column, then soled and heeled a pair of shoes on top.

DUFTON

The village is an Anglo-Saxon settlement, originally formed of simple huts arranged around a broad green. This allowed animals to be corralled, and in later times safeguarded them from border reivers and raiders. In the early 17th century the houses were rebuilt in stone, then further improvements came in the 18th century with the support of the London Lead Company, or 'Quaker Company'. Lead mining ceased in Great Rundale around 1900, but barytes was mined until 1924. More recently the spoil has been worked for fluorspar, which was originally a 'waste' mineral. Facilities in Dufton include the Stag Inn, village store and tea room, youth hostel, and a few bed and breakfasts.

SECTION 3
WARCOP RANGE

One of the largest live military firing ranges in the country is located in the North Pennines, marked on the ground by hundreds of 'danger area' signs around the Warcop Training Area. Public access is extremely limited, and to take advantage of what little access is provided, it is essential to check in advance of a visit. There is a break in live firing on Sunday afternoons, during which time walkers are allowed to use the public rights of way through the range. Certain limited weekends are also available, as well as 'short notice' days that occur with very little advance publicity. The MOD publishes an excellent leaflet explaining the access situation, which can be obtained from the tourist information centre at Appleby, or direct from the MOD.

Three walks are described in this section. The first climbs Murton Pike and Murton Fell, which is outside the 'danger area', but the rest of the walk,

down through Scordale, is inside the 'danger area', and so only available when there is no firing.

Rights of way are followed exclusively through the heart of the 'danger area' over Tinside Rigg, so again, this can only be attempted when there is no firing. The ascent of Mickle Fell is available only if walkers apply for a permit, since there are no rights of way, nor is the bleak moorland designated access land.

Either the little market town of Appleby, or the village of Brough, could be used as bases for exploring this area. Appleby is on the Settle to Carlisle railway line, while buses link both Brough and Appleby with Penrith. Accommodation is available at both places, but Appleby has the greater range of services. Whatever your plans, check first with the MOD, tel 0800 7835181, www.access.mod.uk.

WALK 11
Murton, Murton Pike and Murton Fell

Distance	15km (9¼ miles)
Terrain	A good track leads onto broad moorlands, but the higher parts are pathless and boggy. Good paths and tracks lead down through a rugged dale.
Start/finish	Murton – 729220
Maps	OS Landranger 91; Explorer OL19
Refreshments	None.
Transport	None, but taxis can be hired in nearby Appleby.

The fine viewpoint of Murton Pike can be climbed any time using a right of way. The continuation onto broad and boggy Murton Fell crosses access land and should be available most of the time. However, the descent through Scordale is entirely within the 'danger area' of the Warcop Training Area, and as such, access is limited to no-firing days, and needs to be checked in advance. Scordale is a rugged, deep-cut valley, and well worth a special visit to walk through and explore its lead-mining heritage.

Murton sits on a crossroads and a dead-end road leads to a car park just above the village. Go through a gate onto the open fellside and follow a clear track climbing left, then swinging right, up a slope of friable, ancient, quartz-streaked Ordovician rock. This gives way to limestone at a higher level, overlooking **Gasdale**, where the track bends and features occasional waymark posts.

Watch for a waymark on the left indicating a path leading directly to **Murton Pike**. The summit bears a trig point at 594m (1949ft) and is a fine stance for enjoying views along the East Fellside and across the Vale of Eden to the Yorkshire Dales, Howgill Fells and Lake District.

Double back along the path and continue up the track, until it swings right near a bouldery patch. Don't turn right, but keep straight ahead along a grassy track, still marked as a public bridleway. At some point, leave it and drift gradually right, heading straight up a moorland slope bearing grass, heather, bilberry and cloudberry.

A small, tumbled drystone structure might be spotted before a small cairn is reached around 670m (2200ft) on **Murton Fell**. The broad and bleak summit offers views of the highest North Pennine summits, from Cross Fell to Burnhope Seat, Mickle Fell and Little Fell.

Turn right across the pathless moorland to find a shallow pool, and pass it on either side to reach a line of MOD 'danger area' signs. Only pass these if you have checked that no firing is taking place. Head eastwards in the direction of Mickle Fell. The rugged, boggy slope gives way to easier grassy slopes, then more rugged bog before a broad gap is reached around 600m (1970ft) at the head of **Scordale**.

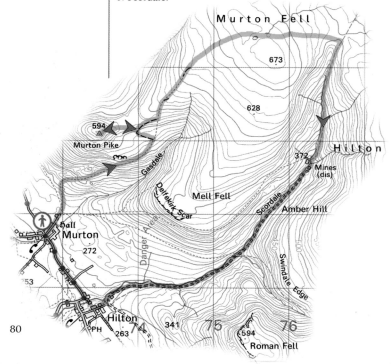

Turn right to walk down into the dale, first following a vague path, then dropping down a little rock-step. Walk down a delightful dry valley, noting how seepage from the surrounding limestone creates a little watercourse later.

Usually, the best footing is on the left-hand side of the stream, but watch out for a marker post and be sure to continue along the right-hand side of the stream. (Although the map shows a right of way consistently on the left, it leads into difficulties, so keep right instead, along a permitted path.)

The path drops steeply and is sometimes vague, keeping above a series of little waterfalls on a steep, rock-strewn slope. A track is joined among the ruins of a lead-mining site, so follow it across the stream and stay on it for the rest of the way through **Scordale**. The river has eaten into one stretch of the track, but apart from that it is plain and easy to follow.

Pass a footbridge, without crossing it, and note that you could switch to Walk 15 at this point, heading up into **Swindale**. Stay on the track and ford a river to continue down the dale.

Murton Pike comes into view on the right, while a grassy track is seen rising to the left. Both the main stony

Looking back along the mining track in Scordale on the descent to the village of Hilton

track and the grassy track lead onwards through gates, joining again as they both leave the 'danger area' at prominent notices. Simply walk straight into the village of **Hilton** and head down through its central green.

Watch for a public footpath signpost on the right, revealing a narrow tarmac path down to Mill Bridge. Cross the bridge, join a road on a corner and walk gently up the road to pass a church and a converted chapel to return to the village of **Murton**.

SCORDALE LEAD MINES

Scordale was developed by the London Lead Company, or 'Quaker Company', who held leases on the lead mines until the 1880s. The dale was equipped with water-powered ore crushers and a smelt mill. A long flue was constructed up the fellside to carry toxic fumes away from the site, and to allow for the collection of condensed substances that would otherwise have been lost. The lowest building in the dale was originally a smelt mill, but when lead mining ceased, it was converted to crush barytes until the 1950s. During the mining years, water in the main streams was polluted. Murton's supply comes from a fellside tank, while clean water at Hilton was dispensed from stone water-points that can still be seen around the village.

WALK 12
Hilton and Tinside Rigg

Distance	18km (11 miles)
Terrain	Good paths, tracks and roads on lower ground, but rugged and sometimes pathless moorland on the higher parts.
Start/finish	Hilton – 735207
Maps	OS Landranger 91; Explorer OL19
Refreshments	None.
Transport	None, but taxis can be hired in nearby Appleby.

This route lies almost entirely within the 'danger area' of the Warcop Training Area, but on most Sunday afternoons, and certain other days in the year, walkers are allowed to follow the rights of way. These run through Scordale and Swindale, across Tinside Rigg and down towards the village of Warcop, allowing an interesting circuit that can be started and finished at Hilton. A sparse but adequate series of waymark posts helps to keep visitors on course – these posts are especially useful on the higher parts around Tinside Rigg where paths are vague.

Start at the top end of **Hilton**, where the tarmac road gives way to a track near a small car park. Follow the track onwards, bending left and right downhill to reach a shelter beside a gate. Ample notices explain about the Warcop Training Area. If no firing is taking place and the red flag is furled, you may proceed, but to avoid disappointment, it is best to check well in advance.

The track runs upstream beside **Hilton Beck**, through another gate and past a limekiln. Stay on the track until a stream has been forded and a junction of tracks is reached.

The village of Hilton is arranged around a fine green equipped with old, stone water points

83

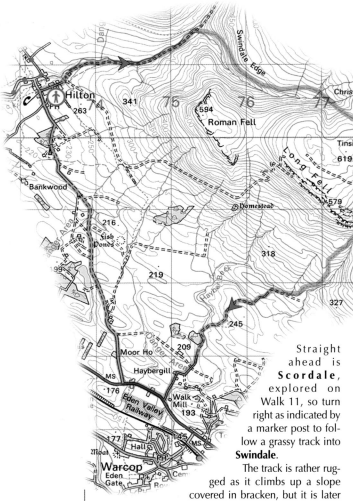

Straight ahead is **Scordale**, explored on Walk 11, so turn right as indicated by a marker post to follow a grassy track into **Swindale**.

The track is rather rugged as it climbs up a slope covered in bracken, but it is later gently graded and covered in short grass. At a higher level it becomes a rugged groove, then it is important to leave it as indicated by a line of marker posts veering off to the right.

Follow these posts carefully, as the path is vague or non-existent, crossing small streams along the way around **Christy Bank**. Looking back through the valley, the northern parts of the Lake District are in view. Keep climbing as marked to cross a bleak moorland gap to the left of **Tinside Rigg**.

Although it is off the right of way, there is unlikely to be any objection to anyone climbing to the summit cairn at 619m (2031ft). Views extend beyond the Vale of Eden to the Lake District, Howgill Fells, Yorkshire Dales, Stainmore and the sprawling high moorland of nearby Little Fell.

To follow the right of way, it is necessary to look carefully down a rugged and pathless moorland slope to pick up a sparse line of waymark posts. Very low outcrops of rock are passed, as well as the squelchy outflow from the little pool of **Dogber Tarn**.

Keep straight ahead uphill to reach a gateway, but do not go through. Instead, turn sharply right to walk away from it and again look out for occasional marker posts. Cross over a grassy track and head down through a pleasant limestone valley.

Cross a step-stile over a fence, where there is a signpost, and continue downhill beside a tumbled drystone wall. Join and follow a grassy track down into a shallow valley, and over to another shallow valley, always following the yellow-topped markers provided.

Tanks use this part of the range, so the track has been reinforced with concrete to avoid them being mired at a river crossing. Cross **Hayber Beck** and follow the track over one last gentle rise to pass **Haybergill**.

A junction is reached with the busy **A66**, and while there are buses between Brough and Appleby, it would be very difficult for them to stop for passengers. Turn right and follow the road with great care until another right turn can be made to leave it. A road is signposted 'Entry no 1 for A B C ranges'. This leads straight through the lower part of the Warcop Training Area to return directly to the village of **Hilton**.

WALK 13
Mickle Fell via the Boundary Route

Distance	12km (7½ miles)
Terrain	High-level, exposed, bleak, remote, pathless, rugged moorlands.
Start/finish	Ley Seat, on the B6276 road – 832199
Maps	OS Landrangers 91 or 92; Explorer OL19
Refreshments	None.
Transport	None.

Access to Mickle Fell, the highest point in County Durham, has always been fraught with problems. The high, rugged, exposed moorlands are difficult underfoot, and bad weather makes any trek to the summit quite arduous. The sprawling moors are used for grouse shooting, part of the fell lies within the Upper Teesdale National Nature Reserve, and the Ministry of Defence has staked out a vast 'danger area'. Those who manage Mickle Fell would prefer walkers to stay away, but walkers go there anyway, and an application can be made for permission to visit by contacting the MOD.

The route described is a straight-up and straight-down walk beside the boundary fence between County Durham and Cumbria, and is referred to as the Boundary Route. Walkers who wish to descend elsewhere must be prepared for a long walk over pathless, rugged, bleak and exposed moorlands.

Assuming you are armed with a permit and that the red warning flag by the cattle-grid on top of the B6276 at **Ley Seat** is safely furled, then you can start this walk along the Boundary Route. Walk northwest from the cattle-grid, following the line of a stone wall. The wall marks the boundary between County Durham and Cumbria. Look out for occasional boundary stones inscribed with numbers – the one nearest to the road being number 46.

The boundary changes direction slightly on the shoulder of **Hewits** at stone number 54, and a fence runs down into the Warcop Training Area to reach **Connypot Beck**.

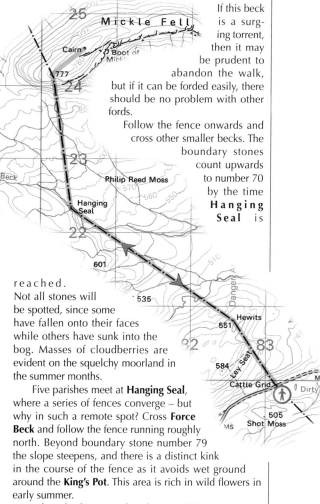

If this beck is a surging torrent, then it may be prudent to abandon the walk, but if it can be forded easily, there should be no problem with other fords.

Follow the fence onwards and cross other smaller becks. The boundary stones count upwards to number 70 by the time **Hanging Seal** is reached. Not all stones will be spotted, since some have fallen onto their faces while others have sunk into the bog. Masses of cloudberries are evident on the squelchy moorland in the summer months.

Five parishes meet at **Hanging Seal**, where a series of fences converge – but why in such a remote spot? Cross **Force Beck** and follow the fence running roughly north. Beyond boundary stone number 79 the slope steepens, and there is a distinct kink in the course of the fence as it avoids wet ground around the **King's Pot**. This area is rich in wild flowers in early summer.

When the fence reaches the top of the steep slope, head off to the right along the broad, grassy, level crest to a large, bouldery cairn marking the summit of **Mickle Fell** at 790m (2591ft). Views are extensive, bleak and desolate, taking in the North Pennines, Yorkshire Dales and the distant fells of the Lake District.

The simplest descent involves retracing steps to Ley Seat. A descent north along the boundary fence can be considered if Maize Beck is running low, allowing a link with the Pennine Way, which could be followed either to Cow Green and Langdon Beck, or to High Cup and Dufton. There are discernible grassy wheel marks that can be traced from the summit of Mickle Fell to the lonely shooting hut of Silverband Shop, where a clear track leads to Holwick.

ACCESS TO MICKLE FELL

Procedure to gain access to the summit of Mickle Fell (taken from a notice posted at Ley Seat).

1 Write to the Range Officer at Warcop Training Area, Warcop, Appleby, Cumbria, CA16 6PA, with the date of your proposed walk, number in the walking party and your proposed route. (Please note: With regret it may not always be possible to grant permission for a walk on certain dates due to constraints imposed by military training, shooting, shepherding or the risk of fire. It may therefore be prudent to provide several possible dates to the Range Officer when writing to him.)

2 The Range Officer will contact all the relevant landowners and gamekeepers on your behalf.

3 A permit and associated regulations will then be issued to you by the Range Officer.

4 Dogs, camping and the lighting of fires are not permitted on this ground.

A series of numbered boundary stones and a fence lead unerringly towards Mickle Fell

SECTION 4
STAINMORE

Stainmore is a forbiddingly broad and bleak tract of moorland that sprawls between the Yorkshire Dales and the North Pennines. Geographically, the southernmost parts of the North Pennines should finish roughly in line with the A66, but the AONB has been stretched all the way across Stainmore to reach the boundary of the Yorkshire Dales National Park. Since prehistoric times, people crossed Stainmore because it was the lowest gap in this part of the Pennines. The Romans were the first to construct a true road over it, but in medieval times it was necessary for travellers to hire guides, while the monasteries established hospices on the route, whose memory is preserved in the placename 'spital'.

Four walks are offered on Stainmore. The first explores very boggy terrain above North Stainmore, in search of an elusive 'slate' quarry. A stretch of Wainwright's Coast to Coast Walk is followed from Kirkby Stephen to the splendid viewpoint of Nine Standards Rigg. Part of the Pennine Way is followed in a circuit from England's highest pub, the Tan Hill Inn. Two other stretches of the Pennine Way are linked on a circuit on Bowes Moor, from the interesting little village of Bowes.

Kirkby Stephen is usually associated with the Yorkshire Dales, but makes a good base for part of the North Pennines, having the greatest range of services in the area. The villages of Brough and Bowes, long bypassed by the busy trans-Pennine A66, offer a little accommodation, food and drink. Bus services over Stainmore are very limited, for those who depend on public transport. Kirkby Stephen is on the Settle to Carlisle railway line and has a bus link with Brough. Bowes, on the other hand, is best approached by bus from Barnard Castle.

WALK 14

North Stainmore and Slate Quarry Moss

Distance	13km (8 miles)
Terrain	Mostly clear tracks and paths on broad, bleak, boggy moorlands, but some pathless terrain too.
Start/finish	North Stainmore – 830151
Maps	OS Landranger 91; Explorer OL19
Refreshments	None. Pubs and café off-route at Brough.
Transport	None, but the Grand Prix bus company at Brough offers a taxi service.

Can there really be a slate quarry high on the boggy moors of Stainmore Common? The map shows a right of way terminating at Slate Quarry Moss, but the underlying rock can't be slate. Investigating on foot requires a walk through appallingly boggy terrain, following a path that is little more than a sodden streak of sphagnum moss and rushes. Evidently this path saw a lot of traffic in its day, suffered as a result and never really recovered. Fortunately, other paths and tracks in the area are much firmer underfoot.

Start in **North Stainmore** beside the uninhabited Punch Bowl Inn, which went out of business after being bypassed by the busy A66. Follow the minor road uphill as sign-posted for Borrowdale Beck, and keep straight ahead at all times, passing a sign that forbids military use of the road. ◀ The road ends at two gates, where there is an 'access land' sign and two signposted public bridleways.

There is a small military training area on Stainmore Common, but they do not use live ammunition and this route does not enter it.

The gate on the left leads to the nearby farm of **Spurrigg End**, so go through the gate on the right instead. Don't follow the stony track to the right, but keep straight ahead along a grassy track signposted for Slate Quarry Moss and go through a gate on the left. Keep following the track uphill and go through another gate. Head downhill to cross a broad wooden bridge over a stream, then climb again and go through another gate.

The track becomes less clear as it crosses a level area of grassy, rushy moorland, then it runs down through a groove and crosses flat rock in the bed of another stream.

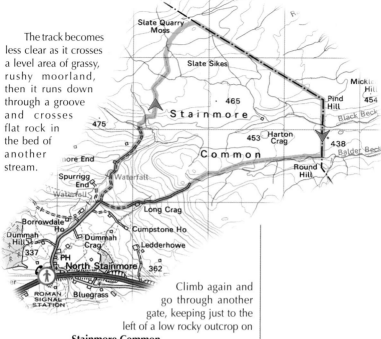

Climb again and go through another gate, keeping just to the left of a low rocky outcrop on **Stainmore Common**.

The track becomes rather vague, but can be identified as a groove full of sphagnum moss and rushes on a rugged grass and heather moor. It is impossible to follow the remains of this track, and best to keep well to the left of it, although the moorland still features a couple of rather alarming streaks of soft sphagnum moss and wobbly 'quaking bogs'.

Tread carefully until a small stream is crossed and firm ground is reached at **Slate Quarry Moss**. Wander gently uphill among low, stony spoil heaps, which are largely grassed over, until the ruins of a stone hut and sheepfold are reached.

SLATE QUARRY MOSS

It is clear that this isn't a true slate quarry, but rather a 'flagstone' quarry, exploiting a very limited outcrop of sandstone. It would have provided slabs thin enough to be used on rooftops, and this would have been cheaper than carting slates from the Lake District. No doubt all the material was used on farm buildings in the immediate area. It is quite likely that the site has been disused for over a century, but the access track has clearly been unable to recover, and was no doubt much worse in its heyday, when horses and carts would have churned the moorland into a morass.

Few walkers would relish backtracking through the awful bog, so it is best to leave Slate Quarry Moss by aiming gently uphill, roughly northeast, to reach a post-and-wire fence that marks the county boundary between Cumbria and Durham, around 510m (1675ft). Turn right to follow the fence in a dead-straight line gently downhill.

A series of boundary stones are passed, numbered in descending order, which count down from 27 or 26, depending on where you hit the boundary fence. The stones were planted every furlong, or eighth-of-a-mile, which equates to every 200m. Quad vehicles have run alongside the fence and left a clear parallel track. Keep an eye on the boundary stones as they count down to number 16 on the rocky hump of **Pind Hill**, where the fence turns suddenly right and there is a stony cairn.

Walk down a rugged moorland slope, still following the fence, but without a clear path. The moorland rises and falls and the stream of **Black Beck** has to be forded. The boundary stones continue their countdown, reaching number 11 just before a gate in the fence at the head of **Balder Beck**. Looking left downstream, the distant, gritstone-capped outline of Shacklesborough can be seen.

Turn right, however, to walk away from the boundary fence, looking for a vague vehicle track on the wet and boggy moorland. The idea is to trace the largely unseen Balder Beck upstream while keeping well away from the flow. A clearer track evolves across **Stainmore Common**, and this is later surfaced with stone as it approaches a gate around 460m (1510ft).

Go through the gate and the track is flanked by dry-stone walls as it heads downhill. Pass the farm at **Long Crag** and go through a gate. Later, a gate gives access to the minor road that was followed earlier in the day, so all that remains is to walk straight downhill to finish at **North Stainmore**.

A fine track leads off Stainmore Common, passing a farm at Long Crag

WALK 15
Kirkby Stephen and Nine Standards

Distance	14km (8¾ miles)
Terrain	Minor roads, tracks and paths lead up from the fields, but the higher moorlands are bleak and boggy.
Start/finish	Kirkby Stephen – 775087
Maps	OS Landranger 91; Explorer OL19
Refreshments	Plenty of choice at Kirkby Stephen.
Transport	Occasional Stagecoach buses link Kirkby Stephen and Kendal, except Sundays. Regular daily Grand Prix buses link Kirkby Stephen, Brough, Appleby and Penrith.

Geographically, Nine Standards Rigg is part of the Yorkshire Dales, but politically, it was excluded from the Yorkshire Dales National Park. When the North Pennines AONB was established, a decision was made to include Nine Standards Rigg and the moors between the national park and the A66. For only an odd feature, few walkers would climb onto this broad and boggy moorland, but for longer than anyone can remember, a curious row of conical cairns has attracted people from far and wide. Over the past few decades these cairns have become more widely known among the countless thousands of people trekking Wainwright's Coast to Coast Walk across northern England.

KIRKBY STEPHEN

The market town of Kirkby Stephen is generally a bustling place that seems more attached to the Yorkshire Dales than the North Pennines, leaving the nearby village of Brough to fulfil the function of a 'gateway' to the North Pennines. Kirkby Stephen is also a major staging post on Wainwright's Coast to Coast Walk, seeing a steady stream of walkers, most of them heading towards Nine Standards Rigg.

Facilities include a range of accommodation options, including a youth hostel in a converted chapel. There are banks with ATMs, a post office, plenty of shops, pubs, cafés and takeaways. There is also a tourist information centre, tel 017683 71199. The railway station outside town is on the celebrated scenic Settle to Carlisle line.

Start in the little market square in **Kirkby Stephen**, in front of the colonnaded entrance to the parish church. The Coast to Coast Walk, which this route follows, goes along a narrow road called Stoneshot, turning left down steps to reach twin-arched Frank's Bridge over the **River Eden**. Turn right to

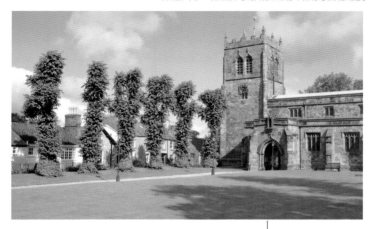

follow a riverside path upstream, then follow a strip of tarmac up through a field to enter the little village of **Hartley**.

Turn right along a road, then left down a short path
to cross a 'clam' footbridge over a wooded stream.
Turn right up another road and pick up another short,
wooded riverside path. Rejoin the road
at a higher level and continue
uphill, avoiding the entrance
to the **Hartley Quarry**. It
is worth turning right
before the quarry to
have a look at a
restored railway
viaduct.

*The parish church in
Kirkby Stephen lies just
off the market square
at the start of the walk*

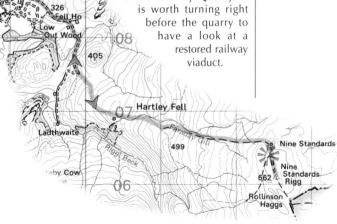

95

Walk up the fell road with ever-widening views, crossing a crest above the quarry. Look ahead to Nine Standards Rigg, as well as further afield to the northern Yorkshire Dales, Howgill Fells, Lake District and the East Fellside flank of the North Pennines. Head down the road and keep well to the right of **Fell House**, then follow the road until the tarmac ends.

Continue along a track and through a gate, then uphill to go through a gateway in a fence. Cross a dip and head uphill again, following a drystone wall and crossing a rise beside a ruined barn. Ford **Faraday Gill**, which cuts through crumbling shale, then climb beside the wall and turn right round a corner.

A signpost indicates a permitted path taking the Coast to Coast Walk directly up open moorland slopes. The path is grassy, but often has a stone foundation, and passes within sight of a drystone sheepfold. Pass a couple of soft and wet patches and aim for the curious row of cairns at **Nine Standards**.

NINE STANDARDS

There should be nine cairns here, largely made up of well-built conical structures, but one of them is a square tower. Occasionally, extra cairns are built by over-enthusiastic visitors, but there seems to be a local reaction against this, resulting in their swift demolition. There is no reliable record as to why the cairns were built. One theory suggests that they were built to make border reivers believe that there was a military camp on top of the hill. Others suggest that they were merely constructed by local shepherds, miners or quarrymen with time on their hands.

Extend the walk a little along the broad and boggy moorland crest to reach a trig point at 662m (2172ft) on **Nine Standards Rigg**. A view indicator stands nearby and the prospect almost extends from coast to coast. Apart from the nearby Yorkshire Dales and North Pennines, the more distant Lake District and North York Moors can be seen. The hump of Criffel in southern Scotland marks

Four of the nine curious cairns that stand on top of Nine Standards Rigg

where the Solway Firth lies, even though it is out of sight, while the smoky chimneys of industrial Teeside mark where the North Sea is located.

The moorlands are access land and walkers are free to head in any direction, but it is all boggy and featureless. The only way to keep feet dry and enjoy a relatively easy walk is to retrace steps back down to Kirkby Stephen.

WALK 16
The Tan Hill Inn and Sleightholme Moor

Distance	14km (9 miles)
Terrain	Rugged, high-level, exposed moorland paths and tracks.
Start/finish	The Tan Hill Inn – 896067
Maps	OS Landranger 92; Explorer OL30
Refreshments	The Tan Hill Inn.
Transport	None.

The Tan Hill Inn is the highest pub in England, standing at a lonely moorland road junction at 530m (1732ft). It was 'transferred' to County Durham during the local government reorganisation of 1974, and this was a sore point with many locals. The pub was brought back into Yorkshire following a boundary change in April 1991.

The Pennine Way passes the inn's door, and this route has in its time been diverted on Sleightholme Moor. Its original course became very boggy, so it was transferred across Frumming Beck onto firmer ground. To create a circular walk, an old bridleway across the moors can be linked with a shooting track and a patchy moorland road. For those who wish to stay longer at Tan Hill, accommodation is available.

Walk out of the porch of the **Tan Hill Inn** and turn left to walk up a minor road and cross a cattle-grid. Turn right along a track, but when the track bends to the right, head off to the left instead.

A path forges across heathery ground that can be boggy in places, and beware of a bell pit just to the left of the path. The route is vague as it crosses the ravine of **Mirk Fell Gill**, but look ahead to spot a low, ruined stone hut and pass to the right-hand side of it.

The path rises past a capped mine shaft and is fairly clear as it crosses **Mirk Fell** at nearly 580m

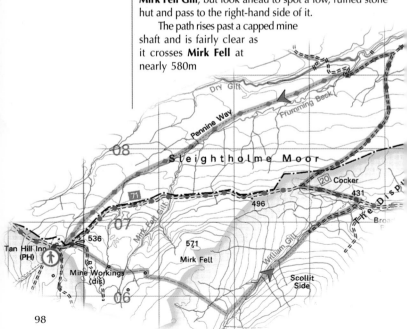

(1900ft). Descend slightly to cross a stream and be sure to continue onwards to the next stream, which is **William Gill**.

While descending towards it, turn left to follow it downstream. A clear track is joined, which crosses and re-crosses the stream using fords and bridges. As the narrow valley begins to widen, the track joins a minor road.

Turn left up the minor road and follow it across the moors. Later, turn right along a patchy road signposted for Bowes (marked as unfit for motors). Follow this moorland road to a junction with a clear track.

Turn left to pass a barrier gate and pass a notice about **Bowes Moor**. The idea is to follow the Pennine Way back towards the Tan Hill Inn. The track crosses a bridge over **Frumming Beck**, then after crossing the bridge, turn left.

Follow a path marked by wooden posts, which keeps well away from the beck, and yet still follows it upstream. Walk mostly on grassy moorland, but beyond some sheepfolds there is more heather cover.

After passing a cairn the path runs closer to the beck in its upper reaches. Aim almost directly for the **Tan Hill Inn**, with the wettest and boggiest stretch coming last. Hit the moorland road just to the left of the buildings, where one stile needs to be crossed before the walk is over.

THE TAN HILL INN

William Camden mentioned an inn at this remote spot in 1586, but the current structure dates from the 17th century. The inn stood at a focal point on packhorse ways and caught the passing trade. Bell pits and open mine shafts dot the bleak moors, and coal mining provided a more regular clientele at the Tan Hill Inn. There is good local support but it relies heavily on tourist traffic, and Pennine Wayfarers seldom pass by if the doors are open. The Tan Hill Inn has featured on television to promote double-glazing, and in foul weather a blazing fire should be burning, but there may be competition for a fireside seat! A variety of accommodation is available, from bed and breakfast to bunkhouse and camping, tel 01833 628246, www.tanhillinn.com.

The Tan Hill Inn is the highest pub in England, on a lonely moorland at 530m (1732ft)

WALK 17

Bowes and Bowes Moor

Distance	16km (10 miles)
Terrain	Easy field paths and farm tracks, with exposed moorland paths.
Start/finish	Bowes – 995135
Maps	OS Landranger 97; Explorer OL31
Refreshments	Pub at Bowes.
Transport	Occasional weekday Central Coaches serve Bowes from Barnard Castle.

This walk over Bowes Moor makes use of the Pennine Way main route and the alternative Bowes Loop. Bowes is a quiet, pleasant little village with a long history of catering for travellers across Stainmore. It is also the site of Dotheboys Hall, which was made notorious by Charles Dickens.

The route leaves Bowes and traces the River Greta upstream to East Mellwaters. By the time God's Bridge is reached, the Pennine Way main route is followed. This crosses desolate Bowes Moor and Deepdale. A short-cut along the moorland crest of Race Yate Rigg enables walkers to transfer onto the course of the Bowes Loop, crossing Deepdale again to return to Bowes.

BOWES

Travellers have crossed Stainmore for thousands of years, as this broad gap on the Pennine moors allows an obvious east–west link. The Romans regulated traffic by constructing a road equipped with forts, camps and signal stations. The fort at Bowes was called Lavatrae, and its square, grassy platform can be discerned, but all its masonry was incorporated into Bowes Castle in 1170. The castle watched over an area that was an unsettled borderland. The Stainmore wastes were bleak, and monastic hospices were established to serve travellers. Memory of these places lingers in the placename 'spital'. A turnpike road was constructed in 1743 and literally paved the way for cross-country coaching, and Bowes still features coaching architecture, such as the Ancient Unicorn pub. The South Durham and Lancashire Union Railway came in 1861, lasting for a century until closure.

Leave **Bowes** by way of the parish church and walk along Back Lane to reach **Bowes Castle**. Turn right to walk beside its perimeter fence and continue through fields to reach a track. Turn left to follow the track and another field path to reach a footbridge over the **River Greta**.

Walk to a farm access road and turn right to follow it to **West Charity Farm**. Turn right and left to pass the farm then cross a footbridge over **Sleightholme Beck** (not the bridge over the Greta). Keep right to follow a path to **East Mellwaters**.

EAST MELLWATERS

Five-and-a-half thousand years of farming history have been excavated around East Mellwaters. Iron Age dwellings were unearthed beside the farm road, as well as a rectangular settlement in a field, a Romano-British house lies across Sleightholme Beck, while the modern farmhouse stands on the site of a medieval dwelling. The farm provides specialist accommodation for people with disabilities, and a network of easy-use trails has been established around nearby fields. Some of these may become rights of way, and other paths may be diverted, so keep an eye out for changes on the way to God's Bridge.

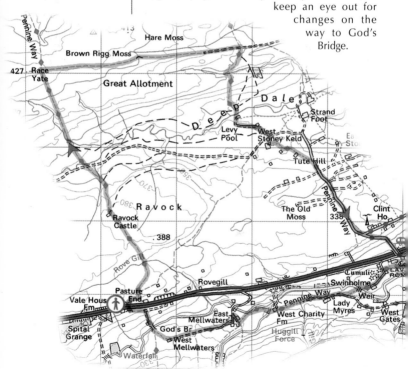

Keep right of the buildings to get onto a farm track running from East Mellwaters to **West Mellwaters**. Go through a gateway just beyond West Mellwaters and bear diagonally to the right to cross a field.

Once over a low rise, head straight down to **God's Bridge**, which is flanked by old limekilns. Cross over the natural limestone slab that forms God's Bridge and follow a track uphill from the river.

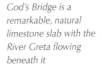

God's Bridge is a remarkable, natural limestone slab with the River Greta flowing beneath it

The busy **A66** is at the top of the track, so divert left and walk beneath the road using an underpass. Turn right on the other side, then left at **Pasture End** to climb up a moorland slope.

Follow a prominent cairned path onwards over a moorland rise, crossing Rove Gill and passing the ruined stone hut of **Ravock Castle**, now piled into a cairn. Wander downhill to cross a track, followed by a footbridge over **Deepdale Beck**. Climb gradually uphill following a wall up the grassy moorland slope.

103

Just before reaching the top of this slope at 427m (1402ft) on **Race Yate**, go through a gate on the right. A track made by wheeled vehicles can be followed across the slopes of **Race Yate Rigg**, and eventually reaches a fence.

Turn right, and although it is tempting to walk alongside the fence, drift to the right away from it. Cross little **Hazelgill Beck**, then use a footbridge to cross Deepdale Beck again at the farm of **Levy Pool**.

Follow the access track up from Levy Pool, joining a tarmac road at **West Stoney Keld**. This leads back to Bowes, but the Pennine Way cuts a bend from it. Walk along the West Stoney Keld access road and turn left before reaching the farm. Follow a field path back to the road and turn right.

The road leads through an old military site flanked by warning signs. Later, turn right to follow another road downhill and cross over the busy **A66**. Walk straight into the village of **Bowes** via Dotheboys Hall, and continue along the main street to the Ancient Unicorn pub.

DOTHEBOYS HALL

Charles Dickens visited Bowes in 1838 and collected material about the notorious Yorkshire Schools, which included Dotheboys Hall. He met William Shaw, the headmaster, who was transformed into the character of Wackford Squeers. Some of Dickens' information was gleaned at the bar of the Ancient Unicorn. The furore raised by the publication of Dickens' work resulted in the ultimate closure of the Yorkshire Schools, to the great relief of their ill-treated inmates. The house is not open to the public.

SECTION 5
LOWER TEESDALE

This section is remarkable in that almost all of it lies outside the North Pennines AONB. Rather than delve into the reasons why it is excluded, perhaps it is better simply to enjoy the region for its own charm and interest. Barnard Castle is an important 'gateway' to the North Pennines, and there are plenty of nearby places that are well worth exploring if using the town as a base. True, the more distant, popular parts of Teesdale may ultimately prove irresistible. The River Tees is deeply entrenched in this area, so riverside strolls can be a little more strenuous than visitors might imagine. This area is also notable for its wealth of trees, which can look stunning in autumn.

Four walks explore the region around Barnard Castle, including two that run close to the River Tees itself. These offer the chance to appreciate the river and its well-wooded surroundings, around Eggleston and Barnard Castle, as well as Cotherstone and Romaldkirk. Another walk, beside the tributary River Greta, is almost like a jungle trek through a wild and well-wooded gorge. The little village of Woodland is rather removed from Teesdale, but it is conveniently included in this section. The quiet countryside around the village was once busy with little collieries and lead mines, whose remains can be discovered on a short and easy walk.

Naturally, Barnard Castle has the best range of services and facilities for anyone visiting this part of the North Pennines, and is also a splendid, historic market town well worth exploring for its own sake. It is an important hub for local bus services, with good connections extending through Teesdale, as well as deep into County Durham to link with the mainline railway at Darlington.

WALK 18
Greta Bridge and Brignall Banks

Distance	13 or 16km (8 or 10 miles)
Terrain	A steep-sided gorge with narrow woodland and field paths.
Start/finish	Greta Bridge – 086133
Maps	OS Landranger 92; Explorer OL30 or OL31
Refreshments	Pub at Greta Bridge.
Transport	Regular Hodgsons buses serve Greta Bridge from Barnard Castle and Richmond, except Sundays.

Before the River Greta reaches its confluence with the mighty River Tees at the Meeting of the Waters, it flows by way of Brignall Banks, through a deep, wooded gorge between Rutherford Bridge and Greta Bridge. Between the bridges the gorge is exceptionally well wooded. Apart from Brignall Mill and the ruins of St Mary's Church, there are no signs of settlement deep in the gorge. The journey through the gorge uses paths on both sides of the river, and is rather like a jungle trek, in contrast to the sheep-cropped pastures at a higher level.

Start on the same side of **Greta Bridge** as the Morritt Arms and walk across the graceful span of the bridge. Pass a fine courtyard building then turn right at a gap between the farm buildings alongside.

Go through a gate, out of the farmyard, and walk across a field before following a path gently uphill through a small wood. Turn right along a minor road then later turn right again round a sharp bend to reach **Wilson House**.

Follow the farm access road from Wilson House to **Crook's House**. Head off to the right before reaching the farm and follow a rather muddy path towards the edge of a wood.

Keep to the edge of the wood until it can be entered at a waymarked gateway, then stay by the inner edge of the wood until the path leads down through the wood to reach the banks of **Gill Beck**. Ford using stepping-stones, which could be difficult when the beck is in spate.

Once across Gill Beck, follow the path uphill and proceed across a steep slope high above the **River Greta**. Part of this path features a safety fence above a steep drop. Later, the path descends and runs upstream, joining a clearer path to reach a footbridge giving access to **Brignall Mill**.

Crossing this footbridge and taking a right turn allows the walk to be shortened, otherwise the route can be extended further upstream to Rutherford Bridge.

To complete the extra distance, don't cross the footbridge, but follow the clear path up to the edge of the wood. Turn right to walk alongside the wood and watch for a path heading back down to the riverside.

Continue upstream, but watch for a path rising gradually up from the woods again, passing through small fields. This path leads to a

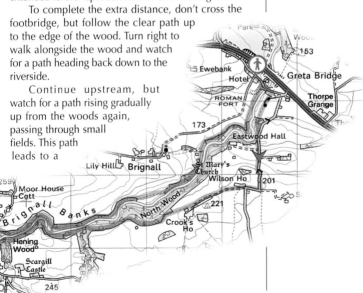

The graceful span of Rutherford Bridge, where the route crosses the River Greta

minor road, which is followed downhill to cross the graceful arch of **Rutherford Bridge**.

Walk uphill a short way on the road, then turn right as indicated by a footpath sign. The path itself is rather vague, but the idea is to keep to the grassy brow above the wooded gorge. **Brignall Mill**, which was seen earlier in the walk, will be noticed before its access track is reached, but the route doesn't go down to the building. (Those who took the short-cut, however, will climb up this track.)

Cross the access track and continue alongside a field until a clear path runs down through the woods to reach the riverside. Follow the path through the wooded gorge, and later emerge into fields to reach the ruins and old graveyard of **St Mary's Church**.

Climb gradually up from the ruins, following a path just outside the woodland edge. Eventually, this path leads down towards **Greta Bridge,** where a stone step-stile leads back onto the road near the Morritt Arms.

BRIGNALL BANKS

Greta Bridge and Brignall Banks attracted poets, writers and artists in the 19th century. Cotman painted a view of Greta Bridge, while Turner painted the nearby Meeting of the Waters. Dickens visited the Morritt Arms while researching *Nicolas Nickleby* and Sir Walter Scott praised the scenery thus:

> *O Brignall Banks are wild and fair,*
> *And Greta woods are green,*
> *And you may gather garlands there,*
> *Would grace a summer queen.*

WALK 19

Barnard Castle and the Tees

Distance	13km (8 miles)
Terrain	Easy, mostly low-level woodland and riverside paths.
Start/finish	Scar Top, Barnard Castle – 049166
Maps	OS Landranger 92; Explorer OL31
Refreshments	Plenty of choice around Barnard Castle.
Transport	Regular daily Arriva buses serve Barnard Castle from Darlington, Bishop Auckland and Middleton-in-Teesdale. There is also a town bus service.

Riverside paths run along both banks of the River Tees and both sides of Barnard Castle, so you can explore the river fully. This walk works its way upstream from Barnard Castle, returning at a higher level to the town. Next, it heads downstream to Abbey Bridge, and offers a chance to visit Egglestone Abbey. Barnard Castle is full of interest and there are many fine buildings in and around the town. The castle dominates the riverside, while Egglestone Abbey and the Bowes Museum occupy commanding ground nearby.

As this walk comes in two halves, with Barnard Castle in the middle, different parts of the town can be explored as the walk progresses, though the Bowes Museum needs plenty of time to visit. In due course you'll be referring to the town as 'Barney', as the local folk do.

Start at Scar Top, which is just off Galgate in **Barnard Castle**, near the castle. Bear right to pass a children's play area and follow a tarmac path downhill. Cross a footbridge over **Percy Beck** (not the large footbridge accompanying the Deepdale Aqueduct, built in 1893).

A cobbly path leads upstream beside the **River Tees**, passing through varied and interesting woodlands, with good ground scrub. Walk beneath towering buttresses that once supported a railway viaduct.

The riverside path is known as the **Rock Walk**, featuring a couple of boulders called the Wishing Stones. Walk between them to get a free wish! After a rise and a descent, the path climbs up a rocky stairway built into a cliff face. Beyond this is a rather muddy stretch of path, before the route leaves the woods and enters a small field.

Look for a gate on the right and follow a short path steeply uphill. Turn right again on top of the slope and follow another path alongside the wood, beside large fields.

Later, go through a gate as marked to walk just inside the wood. The path eventually splits and either way leads back down to **Percy Beck**, but cross it using the lowest footbridge to return to **Barnard Castle**.

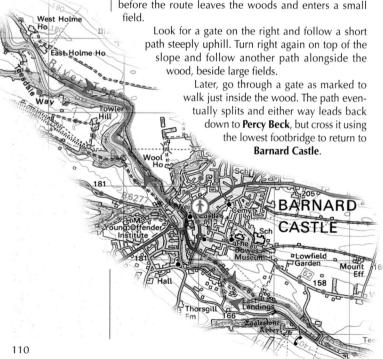

Looking downstream along the River Tees to see
the ruins of Barnard Castle

Either explore the town, or continue with the walk by following a tarmac path between the River Tees and the curtain wall of the castle. This leads down to County Bridge.

Don't cross the bridge, but walk up the main road as if heading into town. However, when the road turns suddenly left, walk straight ahead along Gray Lane. This runs out into the grassy Demesnes, where a track runs beside the **River Tees**.

Follow the track downstream, passing an attractive group of houses and later a sewage works. A riverside path continues through fields, into a small wooded area, before rising to **Abbey Bridge**. Cross this fine arch, then turn right and continue along a minor road.

Egglestone Abbey is worth a visit and is reached by turning left up a road. It was a Premonstratensian foundation, whose construction commenced in 1196. After looking round the ruins, come back down the road and turn left again to pass ancient Bow Bridge.

Look out for a footpath sign on the right, which indicates a field path keeping above the **River Tees** and passing above a caravan site. Later, drop down through the caravan site and turn left along a lane, then right along a path leading to a riverside path again.

Follow this path onto a narrow road, then turn right to cross a footbridge that leads to some old mills across the Tees. Walk straight up Thorngate and continue up past the octagonal market cross to return to Scar Top and Galgate at the top end of **Barnard Castle**.

BARNARD CASTLE

The castle from which Barnard Castle takes its name was built in the 12th century by Bernard Baliol. Its extensive curtain wall stands high above the River Tees at County Bridge. The bridge is not far from a Roman ford and has been altered since being built in 1569, successfully replacing other structures. The market cross around which traffic gyrates is a substantial octagonal building constructed in 1747. Its colonnaded exterior served as a butter market, while the interior has been used as a town hall, courthouse and jail. All facilities are available, including a tourist information centre, tel 01833 690909.

BOWES MUSEUM

Bowes Museum is a remarkable château, commenced in 1860 and funded from the proceeds of the coal industry by John and Josephine Bowes. John was a son of the 10th Earl of Strathmore, while Josephine was a Parisian actress. Between them they amassed an impressive collection of European art to fill the museum. Tel 01833 690606, www.thebowesmuseum.org.uk.

WALK 20
Woodland and Copley

Distance	9km (5½ miles)
Terrain	Easy, low-level field paths and tracks, with some slopes.
Start/finish	Woodland – 075265
Maps	OS Landranger 92; Explorer OL31
Refreshments	Pub at Woodland.
Transport	Weekday Arriva buses serve Woodland from Cockfield, Witton-le-Wear and Bishop Auckland.

Woodland and Copley are at the top of the Gaunless Valley, in an area where several small-scale coal mines once operated, even into the 20th century. A short walk through the area reveals the remains of former industry, with pit spoils, shafts, old tramways and a landmark chimney once linked with a smelt mill at an old lead mine. It is worth having a look at the Gaunless Valley Visitor Centre, located between Butterknowle and Cockfield, beforehand. It contains a wealth of interesting background information about the area.

Start in **Woodland** at the Edge Hotel and walk down the road signposted for Bishop Auckland. Views stretch to the distant North York Moors, to the left, and the North Pennines, to the right. At the bottom of the road, turn left along the farm access road for **Lunton Hill**.

Go through the farmyard and follow the track onwards through fields, then walk downhill by road past **Lynesack Church**. Turn right at the bottom, then, when the road turns left, keep straight ahead instead.

Look for a narrow path enclosed by bushes, which continues through fields to a farmhouse lying upstream beside **Howle Beck**. Turn left to cross the beck, and also cross two access tracks close together while walking a short way uphill.

A footpath marker reveals a way round the right-hand side of a house. Cross fields, looking ahead for a gate and stile, and especially watching for a narrow path running between gardens leading to the road in the village of **Copley**.

The prominent chimney in view carried poisonous fumes from the site, and can be visited by making a short detour off-route, from a car park just across the river.

Cross the road, turning right and immediately left to walk past Chapel Terrace. Head down to **Low Trough Farm** and keep left of it to find a footpath down through fields. This leads down steps on a wooded slope to land on a track just above a house. This was the **Manager's House** for a former lead-smelting mill. ◄

If not visiting the chimney, simply turn right to follow the track through **Cowclose Plantation**. Exit into a field to follow a grassy embankment. Turn right at a gate and walk straight onwards, then left at a gate into **Cowclose**

Wood. Head up from the wood into fields, where the path is vague, but climb and drift to the left.

Pick up a grassy track running through gates, then fork left away from a colliery track and the old Woodland Tramway to cross a footbridge and follow a grassy track. Study a notice about the Cowley Colliery, then walk past the ruins of **Cowley Farm**.

Go through a gateway and turn right, watching for stiles on the way through fields, and cross over two runnels of water on the way up to a farm. The path runs between fences as you turn right to pass the farm, then keep watching for stiles while walking from one farm to another in a straight line.

After passing the last farm, which is **Fold Garth**, cross a field but don't cross a stile ahead. Instead, turn left to climb back to **Woodland**, reaching a road at a corrugated iron church. Turn right along a road to finish at the Edge Hotel.

The route returns to the village of Woodland by way of a corrugated-iron church

WALK 21
Cotherstone and Romaldkirk

Distance	11km (6½ miles)
Terrain	Easy, but occasionally rugged riverside paths and field paths.
Start/finish	Fox and Hounds, Cotherstone – 011198
Maps	OS Landranger 92; Explorer OL31
Refreshments	Pubs at Cotherstone and Romaldkirk. Café off-route at Eggleston Hall.
Transport	Regular daily Arriva buses serve Cotherstone and Romaldkirk from Barnard Castle and Middleton-in-Teesdale.

The long-distance Teesdale Way often uses paths on both sides of the River Tees. Whenever the necessary bridging points allow, circular walks can be enjoyed. The walk round Cotherstone and Romaldkirk is a firm favourite with many walkers. Some paths run close to the River Tees, but there are also paths climbing high above the river, offering extensive views of the surrounding countryside.

Cotherstone and Romaldkirk are attractive, interesting little villages well worth exploring. In between them is the farm of Woden Croft, which was one of the notorious Yorkshire Schools exposed by Charles Dickens. On the opposite side of the River Tees is the notable viewpoint of Percy Mere Rock.

Opposite the Fox and Hounds pub in **Cotherstone**, a narrow road runs steeply downhill and cars can be parked there. Hallgarth Hill, the site of an old castle, overlooks the area.

Turn left to cross a footbridge spanning the **River Balder**, but don't cross a nearby footbridge over the River Tees, which will be crossed at the end of the day's walk. A wooded path leads upstream alongside the **River Tees**, before drifting uphill and away from the river to reach an old walled garden at **Woden Croft**.

Continue past the farmhouse at **Woden Croft**, bearing right while passing the buildings, then stay on a track

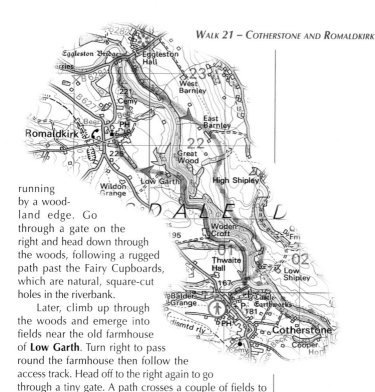

running by a woodland edge. Go through a gate on the right and head down through the woods, following a rugged path past the Fairy Cupboards, which are natural, square-cut holes in the riverbank.

Later, climb up through the woods and emerge into fields near the old farmhouse of **Low Garth**. Turn right to pass round the farmhouse then follow the access track. Head off to the right again to go through a tiny gate. A path crosses a couple of fields to reach an avenue of trees. Turn right at that point to pick up a track leading into the village of **Romaldkirk**.

ROMALDKIRK

This is one of the most attractive and interesting little villages in Teesdale. There are three greens and two pubs, fine cottages and beautiful gardens. An interesting 12th-century church incorporates a little Saxon stonework, and has a couple of unusual features. One is a blocked-up north doorway, said to have the Devil on the other side! Another is the tracery of the east window, which simply doesn't look right. Pevsner declared that it 'looks like a protest against all rules'.

The parish church in the village of Romaldkirk is well worth visiting

An exploration of **Romaldkirk** is recommended, but to continue the walk, turn right and walk past a green, then turn left to walk down a narrow, hedged path. Cross **Beer Beck** and continue over a rise on the field path, then follow the path down to the B6281 near **Eggleston Bridge**. The bridge was built in the 17th century and is thought to have replaced a 15th-century structure.

Cross over the bridge and turn right along a narrow road (but bear in mind that Eggleston Hall and its café lie nearby). The road leads past a small pavilion and ends above a tunnel where water from distant Kielder Reservoir occasionally augments the flow of the **River Tees**.

Just before the tunnel mouth, a stile on the left gives access to a flight of steps climbing up a wooded slope. Emerge into fields on top, then follow a path round the top side of **East Barnley Farm**. The path can be vague afterwards, so look ahead carefully to spot all the necessary waymarks and stiles.

Cross **Raygill Beck** and continue straight across sloping fields to reach the edge of **Shipley Wood**. Later, cross a wall to stand on the top of **Percy Mere Rock**.

PERCY MERE ROCK

The last of the Fitzhughs, who were Lords of Romaldkirk, went out hunting one day and was warned to go home by an old woman. Spurning the warning he continued on his way, and of course should have known better than to hunt anything as unusual as a white deer as night was falling. It was too late to do anything by the time he realised his folly, as he was already plummeting to his death from the precipitous slopes of Percy Mere Rock. The rock provides a wonderful vista, stretching towards desolate Stainmore.

Return to the path and turn right to continue the walk. Later, drop down to the right into a wood and pass through a caravan site. Leave the site and continue down to the **River Tees**.

Cross over a long footbridge, then turn left to cross the footbridge over the **River Balder**, which was used earlier in the day. The nearby road runs straight uphill to **Cotherstone**, emerging opposite the Fox and Hounds.

Looking down on Eggleston Bridge, with Eggleston Hall and its café seen in the distance

119

SECTION 6
MIDDLE TEESDALE

Middleton-in-Teesdale is, as its name suggests, in the middle reaches of Teesdale. Roads converge on the town, so that it can be approached not only by visitors travelling up or down Teesdale, but also those coming from Stanhope, in Weardale, or from Brough, on the far side of Stainmore. For many years this solid little town has welcomed walkers on the Pennine Way, standing between two particularly remote stretches of the route, and those wayfarers passing through the dale always remember it for being charming, easy, restful and scenic.

Three walks are provided from Middleton-in-Teesdale. The first one makes use of an old railway track-bed dating from 1868. Although it was constructed as a mineral line from a series of quarries, it also carried passengers and featured stations at Middleton, Mickleton, Romaldkirk and Cotherstone. All these places are

visited on the walk. Middleton-in-Teesdale was the main headquarters of the London Lead Company, or 'Quaker Company', at a time when the North Pennines was the world's greatest producer of lead. A walk around nearby Monk's Moor reveals extensive ruins associated with the former lead-mining industry. A third walk wanders over to Lunedale and has a completely different theme. The dale was flooded by a series of reservoirs that, along with other reservoirs in the area, were constructed to slake the thirst of rapidly growing towns and industries far removed from Teesdale.

Given the splendid range of facilities available in Middleton-in-Teesdale, it makes a splendid base for exploring all parts of Teesdale. A regular daily bus service reaches the town from Barnard Castle, linking with the little Upper Teesdale bus service for onward progress up through the dale.

WALK 22

Tees Railway Walk

Distance	11km (6½ miles)
Terrain	Easy, low-level walking on a railway trackbed.
Start	Middleton-in-Teesdale – 947254
Finish	Fox and Hounds, Cotherstone – 011198
Maps	OS Landranger 92; Explorer OL31
Refreshments	Plenty of choice around Middleton. Pubs at Mickleton, Romaldkirk and Cotherstone.
Transport	Regular daily Arriva bus services link Middleton, Mickleton, Romaldkirk and Cotherstone with Barnard Castle.

Middleton-in-Teesdale was once served by a branch line from Barnard Castle. It was built as a private concern and opened in 1868, but was taken over by the North Eastern Railway in 1882. The line enabled quarries near Middleton to transport crushed stone out of the dale from quarries biting into the hard Whin Sill. Passenger stations were built at Middleton, Romaldkirk and Cotherstone. The Tees Railway Walk links all three sites and can be used by walkers and cyclists.

As this is a linear route, walkers can catch a bus back to the start if they wish, although the Teesdale Way offers an alternative return along the riverside if a longer walk is desired.

MIDDLETON-IN-TEESDALE

Middleton has 12th-century origins and was close to the hunting and grazing grounds of distant Rievaulx Abbey. The Horsemarket and Market Place point to the settlement's importance in a farming region, and the old market cross and remains of the village stocks survive. Water from Hudeshope Beck powered two corn mills. St Mary's church dates from 1857, but an old arch and detached belfry belong to an earlier church dating from 1557. The churchyard holds the grave of Richard Watson, the celebrated miner-poet

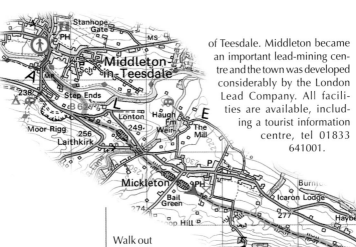

of Teesdale. Middleton became an important lead-mining centre and the town was developed considerably by the London Lead Company. All facilities are available, including a tourist information centre, tel 01833 641001.

Walk out of **Middleton-in-Teesdale** by following Bridge Street, which is signposted as the road for Brough. Cross over County Bridge and turn left down steps to follow a path beside the **River Tees**, then a farm access road.

Pass the farm at **Step Ends** and continue along a track, then follow a path away from the river to reach a road. Turn left along the road, then right along a path, passing a farm at **Lonton** to link with the **Tees Railway Walk**.

Turn left to follow the old railway trackbed, passing fields and quickly crossing a fine, five-arched viaduct over the **River Lune**, constructed in 1848. Cross a road to continue along the trackbed.

When a stone-arch bridge is reached, there is road access to Mickleton, which has two pubs. The old station site is reached next, which also has road access to **Mickleton**.

The trackbed runs easily through pleasant countryside, with views across the breadth of Teesdale. When the route approaches the old station near **Romaldkirk**, climb up to the right, then turn left down a road to reach the village, leaving the trackbed for a while.

ROMALDKIRK

This is one of the most attractive and interesting little villages in Teesdale. There are three greens and two pubs, fine cottages and beautiful gardens. An interesting 12th century church incorporates a little Saxon stonework, and has a couple of unusual features. One is a blocked-up north doorway, said to have the Devil on the other side! Another is the tracery of the east window, which simply doesn't look right. Pevsner declared that it 'looks like a protest against all rules'.

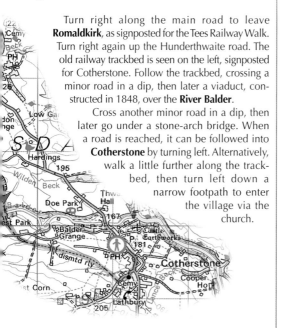

Turn right along the main road to leave **Romaldkirk**, as signposted for the Tees Railway Walk. Turn right again up the Hunderthwaite road. The old railway trackbed is seen on the left, signposted for Cotherstone. Follow the trackbed, crossing a minor road in a dip, then later a viaduct, constructed in 1848, over the **River Balder**.

Cross another minor road in a dip, then later go under a stone-arch bridge. When a road is reached, it can be followed into **Cotherstone** by turning left. Alternatively, walk a little further along the trackbed, then turn left down a narrow footpath to enter the village via the church.

A grassy stretch of the old trackbed runs from Romaldkirk towards Cotherstone

Turn left along the main road to explore the rest of the village, which has a shop and a pub.

COTHERSTONE

Cotherstone is a pretty little village that hardly cares to remember an old castle that once sat on nearby Hallgarth Hill. This 12th-century castle was occupied by the Fitzhughs, who were once the Lords of Romaldkirk.

WALK 23

Middleton and Monk's Moor

Distance	16km (10 miles)
Terrain	Easy woodland and valley paths, then exposed moorland tracks and paths.
Start/finish	Middleton-in-Teesdale – 947254
Maps	OS Landranger 92; Explorer OL31
Refreshments	Plenty of choice around Middleton-in-Teesdale.
Transport	Regular daily Arriva buses serve Middleton-in-Teesdale from Bishop Auckland and Barnard Castle. Upper Teesdale minibuses also serve Middleton-in-Teesdale from Langdon Beck, except Sundays.

A circuit of Monk's Moor reveals lead-mining sites at Hudeshope and Great Eggleshope. Nature is reclaiming the devastated dale-heads, and the once-busy mining paths and tracks are now quiet routes for walkers. Middleton-in-Teesdale was developed and controlled by the London Lead Company and was the headquarters of their Pennine operations. It takes a little imagination to appreciate what the mines would have been like in their heyday, with noisy engines, crushing mills, sterile spoil heaps and polluted waters. Hard work and loyalty to the company was rewarded with good housing, a decent wage and prospects for improvement.

This route starts at an ornate black-and-yellow drinking fountain erected in honour of a past company superintendant.

Walk out of **Middleton-in-Teesdale** by following the road signposted for Stanhope that runs uphill from the parish church. Note an old arch in the graveyard while passing the church.

A narrow tarmac road branches left of the Stanhope road, and after a short walk along it, the **King's Walk** heads off to the right. This permitted path runs through delightfully mixed woodlands. Follow it along the wood-land edge, turning right to climb uphill, then bear right at junctions to cross **Snaisgill Beck** using a footbridge. Follow the woodland edge down to a good track and look at the Skears Limekilns.

SKEARS LIMEKILNS

These kilns were built between the early 18th and mid-20th centuries and operated until 1960. Limestone was quarried and crushed, then trans-ported by a short railway to the kilns. Layers of limestone and coke were fired at 1000°C to make quicklime. 1000kg (1 ton) of limestone and 200kg (4cwt) of coke produced 650kg (13cwt) of quick-lime. This was mainly for fertilising fields, but also produced mortar for construction and was used in lead smelting.

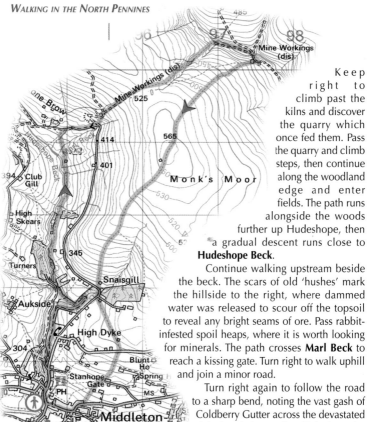

Keep right to climb past the kilns and discover the quarry which once fed them. Pass the quarry and climb steps, then continue along the woodland edge and enter fields. The path runs alongside the woods further up Hudeshope, then a gradual descent runs close to **Hudeshope Beck**.

Continue walking upstream beside the beck. The scars of old 'hushes' mark the hillside to the right, where dammed water was released to scour off the topsoil to reveal any bright seams of ore. Pass rabbit-infested spoil heaps, where it is worth looking for minerals. The path crosses **Marl Beck** to reach a kissing gate. Turn right to walk uphill and join a minor road.

Turn right again to follow the road to a sharp bend, noting the vast gash of Coldberry Gutter across the devastated dale-head. Immediately before the sharp bend is a mining track on the left. Follow this uphill, noting that it swings sharply right, then left. (A public footpath is sign-posted straight uphill, if you wish to follow it.)

On the right there is another track, passing through a gate and leading over from **Hudeshope** to Great Eggleshope. This is a plain and obvious track, crossing moorlands as high as 540m (1770ft). There are small mining remains along the way.

The descent into **Great Eggleshope** is less apparent, so keep to the left of a small beck to avoid difficult ground. Watch for a small ruin on top of a spoil heap, and keep to the left of it to find a path leading to a stile in a wall.

Turn right at the foot of the slope and go through a gate to pick up a track that follows **Great Eggleshope Beck** downstream. Ford this river then later cross a concrete slab bridge. Just before reaching a couple of derelict buildings, turn right and climb straight uphill.

A vague path leads to an old bell pit beside a stone wall. Cross a stile and head straight up a moorland slope. Actually, it is better to bear slightly right to exploit a grassy strip and keep off the heather. Pass to the right of a small, breached dam. Pass a white porcelain sink, and as height is gained, drift slightly left.

When a big cairn is seen on the rocky edge of **Monk's Moor**, keep well to the left to reach another cairn. A vague path runs past it, crossing the top of the moor at 565m (1855ft). However, this is all access land, and it is worth visiting the big cairn and walking along the rocky edge, passing an intricate sheepfold and a ruined shooting hut.

When heading roughly southwest down from Monk's Moor, note a line of grouse butts, and well to the left, a solitary cairn on a boulder. Pick a way between the butts and cairn, exploiting a grassy strip, and walk down to a wall. Turn left to follow the wall to a junction and cross a stile.

Look ahead to spot wheel marks on the grassy slopes of **Brown Dodd**, leading down through a gate and eventually to a road. The right of way actually turns left before reaching the road, but it hardly matters, since this is still access land. Turn left along the road, which then bends right at **Snaisgill**.

Watch for a public footpath signpost on the left and cross a stile into a field. Head diagonally up the field to spot the next stile, then look ahead to spot other stiles in and out of fields, crossing a rise and heading down past a barn to a road.

An old farmhouse is passed on the way from Snaisgill to Middleton-in-Teesdale

Cross the road and walk downhill beside another field. Keep to the right of a farm at **Stanhope Gate**, then follow the course of a very small beck downstream to locate the necessary stiles and gates leading down to a road below. Turn right to follow the road straight back into **Middleton-in-Teesdale**.

THE LONDON LEAD COMPANY

The London Lead Company, or 'Quaker Company' after the religious persuasion of its directors, dominated mining activities in Teesdale and far beyond. This region was formerly the world's greatest producer of lead, and the company provided a stable continuity of employment and development for two centuries, from the 1700s to the 1900s. The company superintendent lived in grand style at Middleton House, while loyal employees could expect good accommodation and access to education and other services. At one time 90 per cent of Middleton's working population were employed directly by the company. Cottages on California Row were built after a large deposit of lead was discovered in 1849, the same year as the California gold rush.

A town trail reveals the former blacksmith's shop, corn mill, school and co-op. New Town was developed as a model housing estate. When Robert Bainbridge retired from the position of company superintendent, a public subscription raised the ornate black-and-yellow drinking fountain in the town. The fountain has a twin at the mining village of Nenthead in Cumbria.

WALK 24

Middleton and Grassholme

Distance	14km (9 miles)
Terrain	Fairly good hill paths, then easy, low-level paths.
Start/finish	Middleton-in-Teesdale – 947254
Maps	OS Landrangers 91 or 92; Explorer OL31
Refreshments	Plenty of choice around Middleton-in-Teesdale. Café at Grassholme Reservoir.
Transport	Regular daily Arriva buses serve Middleton-in-Teesdale from Bishop Auckland and Barnard Castle. Upper Teesdale buses also serve Middleton-in-Teesdale from Langdon Beck, except Sundays.

There are more paths and tracks for walkers than most maps care to admit. The Pennine Way, well known as the first of Britain's waymarked long-distance trails, runs between Middleton-in-Teesdale and Grassholme. Other routes are available as permitted paths, including a shoreline path beside Grassholme Reservoir and the trackbed of the Tees Valley Railway. A combination of all these routes offers an interesting, short circular walk.

The shore of Grassholme Reservoir is one of many reservoirs opened to the public by Northumbrian Water, while the Tees Valley Walk along the old railway trackbed is one of several railway paths opened up for public use in the North Pennines.

Walk out of **Middleton-in-Teesdale** by following Bridge Street, which is signposted as the road for Brough. Cross over County Bridge and go uphill a short way before turning right along a road signposted for Holwick.

Immediately on the left is a Pennine Way signpost. Follow a track uphill, crossing an old railway trackbed to climb to a gate. Keep right and climb up a grassy track to cross the crest of **Harter Fell**, well to the right of a landmark clump of trees on Kirkcarrion.

KIRKCARRION

The dark clump of trees on Kirkcarrion is like a pivot to this circular walk. The trees are said to cover the tomb of a Brigantean prince called Caryn. The tomb was excavated in 1804 and an urn of charred bones was discovered. The site has a mysterious atmosphere and is reputed to be haunted.

*Five-arched
Grassholme Bridge*

Pass through a wall on the crest of **Harter Fell**, then note that the descent can be a bit fiddly. Aim for a ruined barn and keep left of it, then go down to another barn and keep right of it. The farm of **Wythes Hill** lies across a shallow valley, and all the necessary gates and stiles fall into place if the small fields are crossed diagonally.

Pass the farm and follow its access road down to the **B6276**. Another path starts just across the road and runs down through fields to reach **Grassholme Farm**. Turn left on leaving the farm to follow a minor road across **Grassholme Bridge**. ▶

Climb steeply uphill from the reservoir, but only a short way, then turn left through an iron gate to enter the enclosure of **Grassholme Reservoir**. A pleasant shore walk runs between the reservoir and its stout boundary wall, and all the inflowing becks have footbridges.

When the dam of the reservoir is reached, pop into the **Grassholme Visitor Centre** to learn more about the history of and technical background to water catchment and supply, as well as taking in details about conservation in the area. A café is also available.

After a prolonged dry spell the ruins of an old double-arched stone bridge are seen amid mudflats.

TEESDALE RESERVOIRS

The first reservoir built in this area was Hury Reservoir. Construction began in 1884 in response to a huge increase in the population of Middlesbrough. Blackton Reservoir was completed in 1896, then work began on Grassholme Reservoir in 1910. Construction spanned 14 years and a tunnel was built to link with Hury Reservoir. Between 1950 and 1970, Selset Reservoir, Balderhead Reservoir and Cow Green Reservoir were built. Water from Lunedale and Baldersdale flows down pipelines to the Lartington Treatment Works, then is piped to consumers in Teesdale, Darlington, South Durham and Cleveland. Water from Cow Green simply regulates the flow of the River Tees and water is abstracted far downstream at Broken Scar near Darlington, where it may be mixed with water from Lartington. Untreated water is abstracted from the Tees even further downstream at Blackwell and Yarm for industrial use. Kielder Water's reserves can be used to augment the flow of the Tees via a subterranean aqueduct to the river at Egglestone.

Follow the access road up from the **Grassholme Reservoir** dam and turn left along a minor road. A short road-walk leads to a signposted road junction, while on the left there is a footpath signpost. There is no trodden path across the field, so note the direction in which the sign points.

Go through the second gateway downhill, on the right, through a wall beside the first field, then follow the wall downhill. Go through a gate at the bottom and cross stone slabs over tiny **Eller Beck**. Turn right to go through another gate then walk uphill to **Westfield House** and continue along its access road.

Turn right to walk down a narrow tarmac road until a splendid five-arched railway viaduct comes into view. Turn left to walk across it, following the **Tees Railway Walk**. Continue along the old railway trackbed through a pleasant cutting. Turn right as indicated by a sign for Middleton and pass a farm at **Lonton** to reach a road.

Turn left along the road, then right to pick up a field path leading to the **River Tees**. Follow the riverside path upstream, past a farm at **Steps End**, to reach County Bridge. Turn right to walk back up into **Middleton-in-Teesdale**.

Upper Teesdale is one of the most fascinating parts of the North Pennines – a wonderfully green landscape of high-altitude meadows, famous for their range of wild flowers. Black-and-white farmsteads are dotted around the dale, while the River Tees describes sweeping meanders, broken at intervals by some of the most powerful waterfalls in the country. Low Force, High Force and Cauldron Snout are the most famous, but there are many more to be discovered. The Pennine Way has introduced many walkers to the delights of Upper Teesdale, while the extensive Moor House and Upper Teesdale national nature reserves protect the unique ecosystems of the area.

Five routes are described in Upper Teesdale, first taking a relatively easy stroll beside the River Tees to admire Low Force and High Force. An altogether longer and more rugged walk wanders far over bleak and remote moorlands, crossing from Teesdale to Lunedale and back again via Hagworm Hill. A shorter walk crosses the rugged hump of Cronkley Fell, which is home to notable plant communities that thrive on the peculiar 'sugar limestone' on top of the fell. An easier circuit explores similar terrain around Widdybank Fell, starting and finishing at Cow Green Reservoir. A final circular walk, also from the reservoir, wanders further round the moorland slopes of Herdship Fell.

Facilities in Upper Teesdale are spread thinly among small villages or mere hamlets. However, there are various accommodation options, along with a few pubs offering food and drink. The little Upper Teesdale bus operates daily, except Sundays, between Middleton-in-Teesdale and Langdon Beck. If advance notice is given, this bus will provide drop-offs and pick-ups at Cow Green and Holwick.

WALK 25
Low Force and High Force

Distance	13km (8 miles)
Terrain	Easy riverside paths, with moorland paths and tracks.
Start/finish	Bowlees Visitor Centre – 907283
Maps	OS Landrangers 91 or 92; Explorers OL19 and OL31
Refreshments	Café at Bowlees Visitor Centre. Pub and restaurant off-route at Holwick.
Transport	Upper Teesdale buses serve Bowlees from Middleton-in-Teesdale and Langdon Beck, except Sundays.

The waterfalls of Upper Teesdale are truly magnificent. High Force is England's biggest waterfall, where the Tees breaks furiously over a dolerite cliff. Low Force is a less powerful, but attractively rugged cascade. Both waterfalls are easily approached from the B6277, and many casual visitors link them by following a riverside path that is part of the Pennine Way.

If the walk from Low Force to High Force is extended, then Bleabeck Force can be included further along the Pennine Way. To create a circular walk, the Pennine Way can be linked with the course of the Green Trod on Cronkley Fell to return to the village of Holwick. Low Force is seen a second time this way and there is the option, if starting and finishing at Bowlees, to include the nearby waterfall of Summerhill Force.

BOWLEES VISITOR CENTRE

Housed in an old Methodist chapel, the Bowlees visitor centre offers background information and displays relating to the geology, history and natural history of Teesdale. There are plenty of notes about wild flowers, and some species may actually be growing in planted areas outside the building. There is helpful literature on sale, including plant guides specifically about the flowers of Upper Teesdale. There is a small café on site, tel 01833 622292.

Walk away from **Bowlees** and its visitor centre to cross the B6277. A field path leads to a wood, then drops down to cross the **Wynch Bridge**, a suspension footbridge.

THE WYNCH BRIDGE

This was the site of the earliest suspension bridge in the country, strung across the gorge in 1704. It collapsed and was replaced with the present structure. During a flood in recent years it was possible to lie down on the footbridge and touch the surface of the river beneath!

Once across the bridge, turn right to follow the Pennine Way upstream alongside the **River Tees**, passing a sculpture of sheep and admiring waterfalls at **Low Force**.

There are other small falls and rocky gorges further upstream, then **Holwick Head Bridge** is passed and a short climb leads up through a gateway. The Pennine Way is surrounded by profuse growths of juniper as it continues upstream, and this is said to be the largest stand of juniper in the country.

Although the path is hemmed in by juniper, the roar of **High Force** is heard on the approach, and spur paths lead off to the right to precarious viewpoints.

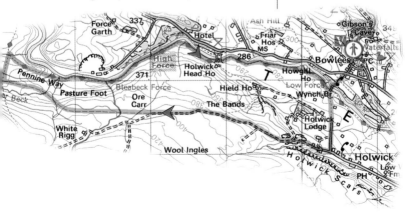

A gentle stretch of the River Tees between Low Force and High Force

HIGH FORCE

Enjoy the sight of the water pounding furiously over a rock-step and boiling in a turbulent pool before rushing through a deep and rocky gorge. This is all seen for free, while people down in the gorge have paid for access from the High Force Hotel.

Continue along the course of the Pennine Way, passing close to the top of **High Force** and heading through an area sparsely clothed in juniper. A noisy, dusty quarry lies opposite the waterfall of **Bleabeck Force**, which is itself seen on the left.

After inspecting this charming little fall, continue along the path, crossing small footbridges and climbing uphill through an area of juniper that has been fenced.

The Pennine Way features flagstone paving in some parts. Watch for the point where the Pennine Way swings north, and turn left, or south at that point. A vague path beside a fence leads across a beck by a gateway.

Just beyond is the **Green Trod**, which is a prominent, grassy ribbon of a track across rough moorland. A national nature reserve sign confirms that this is the right place. Turn left and follow the Green Trod gently downhill.

Cross a couple of becks and climb more steeply uphill alongside a wall.

Later, cross **Blea Beck** using stepping-stones. Pass a cairn on a knoll and turn left along a clear track flanked by fences. Later, turn right to cross a stile flanked by sheep sculptures, and follow another track dropping down into a rocky valley at **Holwick Scars**.

The track reaches a minor road just on the edge of the village of **Holwick**. Turn left to take the road away from the village, then at the next bend use a field path on the right to descend to Low Force and the **Wynch Bridge**. Cross the footbridge and walk up through a wood to cross a field. Cross the B6277 and follow a minor road straight towards **Bowlees** and its visitor centre.

To see yet another waterfall, follow a nearby riverside path upstream from a car park. This runs along a firm surface and soon reaches Gibson's Cave – an overhanging lip of rock where **Summerhill Force** pours into a broad pool. Afterwards, retrace steps to the visitor centre to finish.

WALK 26

Holwick and Hagworm Hill

Distance	24km (15 miles)
Terrain	Rugged, high-level, bleak and exposed moorlands, sometimes with vague paths.
Start/finish	Holwick – 904270
Maps	OS Landrangers 91 or 92; Explorers OL19 and OL31
Refreshments	Pub and restaurant at Holwick.
Transport	Upper Teesdale buses will, by prior arrangement, run between Middleton-in-Teesdale and Holwick.

The sprawling slopes of Mickle Fell could be said to extend from Brough in Cumbria's Eden Valley to Middleton-in-Teesdale in County Durham, and from Cow Green Reservoir to Lunedale. This is an immense area of bleak moorland with very restricted access at its heart. However, footpaths and bridleways may be followed almost any time and some parts are designated access land.

This route starts and finishes in the little village of Holwick, but is long and remote, with no useful facilities along the way. The Green Trod is followed from Holwick to Cronkley, then a footpath leads over the moors from Cronkley to Hargill. The B6276 is used in Lunedale, then a bridleway is followed from Wythes Hill back to Holwick. This represents a long and hard moorland walk, best attempted in fine weather when plenty of time is available. Some paths are vague or lightly trodden so navigation needs to be good.

Holwick is a long and straggly village. Walk through it until the road suddenly turns right, and go straight through a gateway flanked by a bridleway signpost. A track rises up through a rocky valley at **Holwick Scars**, where clumps of parsley fern grow in abundance.

The track turns to the right towards the top of this valley. Cross a stile flanked by sheep sculptures, then follow another track off to the left, fenced on both sides and climbing gently across the moors.

A signpost beside a gate suddenly indicates a point where a public bridleway veers off to the right. (Looking at a map, it seems sensible to continue along the stony track, which provides a short-cut, and normally there will be no objection to this, since it crosses access land.) The bridleway, however, follows the **Green Trod**, which is a vague moorland path that leads through another gate.

Pass a cairn on a knoll above a noisy stone quarry, then follow a drystone wall across a broad dip to cross stepping-stones over **Blea Beck**. The track climbs over a low rise, then descends steeply alongside a wall and crosses a couple more becks.

A gentle ascent leads to a national nature reserve sign. Turn left and ford **Skyer Beck** at this point, through there is no trodden path across the moor. Climb uphill and keep to a slight break of slope to the left-hand side of the steepest parts of **Noon Hill**. The patchy moorland has been selectively burnt, and the route runs roughly southwards across it.

Cross over the stony track that was being followed earlier, or if you arrive via the stony track, then turn left instead. Either way, step across **Dry Beck** onto the moor. There is no discernible path across the grass and heather moor, but there are a few waymark posts, and a national nature reserve sign indicates that the correct course is being followed.

Dry Beck is forded on a broad and pathless stretch of moorland near the Green Trod

Look south across **Howden Moss** to spot a grassy ribbon of a path climbing towards Hagworm Hill. Walk towards this and climb uphill between **Blea Beck** and the line of a fence. A couple of cairns stand on the minor bump of **Hagworm Hill** at almost 600m (1970ft).

The grassy ribbon of a path leads downhill from a corner on the fence, then the heathery moorland slope becomes more stony on the way towards a tall and slender cairn. Keep an eye on the course of the path, which is vague in places, and it gradually it makes its way down to the confluence of Hargill Beck and Green Grain.

Turn right to ford **Hargill Beck** and follow a track uphill. This levels out and a vague path leads towards a large shed beside the **B6276**. ▶

Variant: It is possible to follow the track instead directly to the road without fording the beck.

139

Turn left to follow the road across **Hargill Bridge**, then pass through woodlands at **Wemmergill Hall**, which offers accommodation. Continue past an old chapel, then a quarry where **Robin Hood's Stone** might be seen. Pass a telephone box to find the farm access road for Wythes Hill nearby on the left.

Walk up the access road, which is part of the Pennine Way. Turn left at **Wythes Hill**, then pass another building behind the farmhouse, before leaving the Pennine Way by turning left through a gate.

Walk uphill alongside a wall, following a tractor track through a couple more gates, fording **Merry Gill** to climb past a ruined stone hut, keeping to its left. Walk uphill, using the course of a grassy track to cross **Scarset Rigg**. The track descends slightly to a couple of small black huts, where a left turn leads up a stonier track.

While heading towards the hump of **Green Fell**, be sure to bear to the right. A vague path runs across its slopes towards an area known as **Stone Houses**. It is possible to overshoot the point at which a descent should be made from the 500m (1650ft) contour, but this is no problem, since a wall runs down to a point where a gate allows **Rowton Beck** to be crossed.

A narrow path runs down a moorland slope to a gate in a fence. Go through the gate and follow a clear path flanked by numerous cairns. Follow this path through another gate, then drift to the right down through a rocky valley at **Holwick Scars**. Again, parsley fern grows abundantly on the boulder slopes.

Cross the steep-sided rocky valley and turn right along a track to return to **Holwick** to bring this long moorland walk to a close.

HOLWICK

Holwick is a sturdy little village that was once the most northerly village in Yorkshire before being annexed to County Durham. At the start of the walk, it may be possible to catch a glimpse of Holwick Lodge, which was built in the late 19th century. It looks palatial and is used by grouse-shooting parties, and is said to have been used by the late Queen Mother on her honeymoon. The Strathmore Arms offers food, drink, accommodation and camping. Low Way Farm offers food and drink at the Farmhouse Kitchen, as well as a nearby bunkhouse barn and camping.

WALK 27
Cronkley Fell

Distance	12km (7½ miles)
Terrain	Some good tracks, but also exposed moorland paths and a rugged riverside path.
Start/finish	Forest-in-Teesdale – 867297
Maps	OS Landrangers 91 or 92; Explorer OL31
Refreshments	None.
Transport	Upper Teesdale buses serve Forest-in-Teesdale from Middleton-in-Teesdale, except Sundays.

Cronkley Fell is a mere bump on the wild, broad, sprawling slopes of Mickle Fell. It is managed as part of the Upper Teesdale National Nature Reserve, and a series of fenced plots across the top of the fell contain a wealth of rare and uncommon flowers. The fell can be approached from Forest-in-Teesdale, by using a short stretch of the Pennine Way. A grassy track known as the Green Trod leads over the higher parts of the fell, then a rugged path beside the River Tees can be used to return to Forest-in-Teesdale. If information about the range of flowers in Upper Teesdale is required in advance of this walk, then go to the Bowlees visitor centre (see Walk 25).

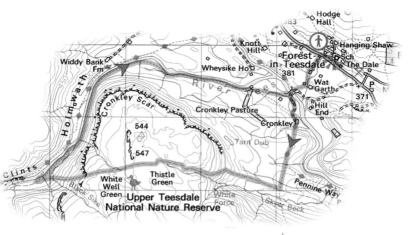

Forest-in-Teesdale is a sprawling settlement, no more than a few farms and houses scattered among fields. The Upper Teesdale Bus serves the area and passes a car park below a school and a farmhouse bed and breakfast.

Starting from the car park, turn right along the main road to spot a footpath sign, then turn left to follow a field path straight down towards a farm, keeping right of the building to continue down to the **River Tees**. A farm access track crosses a bridge and leads to **Cronkley Farm**, following the course of the Pennine Way.

Climb a rugged path behind the farm and cross a gentle rise, followed by a dip. The Pennine Way climbs

The Green Trod is a grassy ribbon of a track across rugged moorland, climbing onto Cronkley Fell

143

gently uphill then swings left downhill. Don't follow it, but keep straight ahead, following a vague path beside a fence to cross a beck by a gateway. Just beyond is the **Green Trod**, which is a prominent, grassy ribbon of a track across rough moorland. A national nature reserve sign stands beside it.

Turn right to follow the track uphill, and later pass a sign announcing open access. The track leads over the broad top of **Cronkley Fell**, passing a series of fenced enclosures. These protect wild flowers growing on 'sugar limestone' from grazing by sheep and rabbits.

Pass a spring at **White Well** and walk down past a cairn to follow a path down to the **River Tees**. A fenced enclosure has been planted with juniper, and an island in the river is covered in it.

THE TEESDALE ASSEMBLAGE

The peculiar range of flowering plants thriving in Upper Teesdale owes its existence to a number of factors. The arctic/alpines survive because the climate in this bleak region suits them, keeping taller and more competitive plants at bay. The underlying crumbling 'sugar limestone' suits some species, while others grow on sodden, acid peat bogs. Plants that once grew in well-wooded areas now survive by adapting to life in the shade of boulders and cliffs. Many hear about the spring gentian, which is strikingly blue on sunny days in early summer, though few know exactly where to find it. Other species of note include the mountain pansy, alpine bistort, bird's-eye primrose, Teesdale violet and blue moor grass. These grow alongside more commonplace wild thyme, tormentil, thrift and harebells, while wood anemones and woodland ferns have adapted to non-wooded habitats. The plants of the Teesdale Assemblage are survivors from a bygone age, but also remind visitors how habitats have changed over long periods of time.

Turn right to walk downstream. At first there is plenty of space for the path, but later the ground is rugged and the path narrow. Boardwalks have been installed in some places around the foot of **Cronkley Scar** and there are views across the river to Widdybank Farm.

The path becomes wider and easier, passing a tumbled stone ruin. Continue to reach a barn and go through gates to pass it. Follow a path through a field to reach a bridge that was crossed at the start of the day's walk. Cross it again and retrace your steps up through fields to return to the car park below the school at **Forest-in-Teesdale**.

WALK 28
Cow Green and Widdybank Fell

Distance	16km (10 miles)
Terrain	Easy, though remote, roads and good paths.
Start/finish	Cow Green – 810308
Maps	OS Landrangers 91 or 92; Explorer OL31
Refreshments	None closer than the Langdon Beck Hotel.
Transport	Upper Teesdale buses, operating from Middleton-in-Teesdale and Langdon Beck, except Sundays, will run to Cow Green if booked in advance.

Widdybank Fell is an easy area to approach in search of Upper Teesdale's rare flowers. The walk round the fell uses minor roads and the course of the Pennine Way. Cow Green Reservoir dominates the start and finish, and while it is now part of the scenery, its construction caused howls of protest.

The spectacular waterfall of Cauldron Snout is a fine feature on this route. Walk round Widdybank Fell on a sunny day in the middle of May to make the most of its floral tributes. The spring gentian is at its best around that time, and there are many more plants to see. Notice the outcrops of 'sugar limestone', which breaks down to form a crumbly soil that many of these plants prefer. Look for more wild flowers growing around the hay meadows of Widdybank Farm, which aren't mown until late in the summer.

COW GREEN RESERVOIR

Cow Green Reservoir was constructed to slake the thirst of Teesmouth and its burgeoning industries. Sadly, an area rich in rare plants was drowned, despite vociferous protests, though some last-minute transplantation took place. The dam was built between 1967 and 1970 and holds 41 million cubic metres of water (9000 million gallons). The surface of the water covers 310 hectares (770 acres) and is 489m (1603ft) above sea level. Water is not piped away, but merely impounded and released as required, so that the flow of the River Tees can be regulated, allowing water to be abstracted far downstream at Broken Scar, for domestic use, and at Blackwell and Yarm, for industrial use.

Start at the **Cow Green** car park, checking information boards that display basic facts about the geology, scenery, flora and fauna of Upper Teesdale. Follow a nearby **nature trail**, which starts as a firm pathway, but later

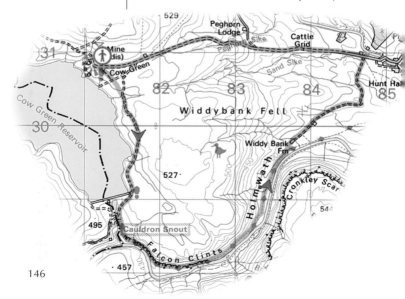

follows the narrow minor road down past the enormous **Cow Green Reservoir** dam. ▶

Don't cross the bridge spanning the **River Tees** below the dam, but turn left along a flagged pathway to descend alongside **Cauldron Snout**, using the Pennine Way. A narrow gorge has been cut by the river, and the water boils furiously as it beats against the walls and tumbles over rock-steps.

Step down carefully alongside, noting that the rock can be slippery when wet, and has been polished by the boots of previous visitors. Stand still if you want to admire the falls, then after a final pyramidal outpouring, the Tees spreads out across a bouldery bed and rushes round a corner on its way to High Force (see Walk 25).

The path continues as a flagged pathway hemmed in between the River Tees and the cliffs of **Falcon Clints**. Ironically, the flagstones were quarried from the Pennines and used to build a mill that was later demolished, with the stone being 'recycled' back into the Pennines.

Later, wooden boardwalks prevent boggy ground from becoming over-trodden. As the cliff line dwindles, **Cronkley Scar** rears up on the opposite side of the River Tees. **Widdybank Farm** comes into view – one of the most remote farms in the region.

In spring and early summer, inspect the springy turf on the crumbling 'sugar limestone' beside the road, which supports a variety of wild flowers.

The Pennine Way passes the cliffs of Falcon Clints on the way to Widdybank Farm

WIDDYBANK FARM

Haymaking comes late around Widdybank Farm, compared to farms further down Teesdale, owing to the altitude and resulting lower temperatures. Flowers growing in this area have a chance to ripen and drop their seeds before mowing takes place, resulting in self-regenerating, species-rich meadows. The farm is a base for Natural England staff working on the Moor House and Upper Teesdale national nature reserves.

Follow the access road away from **Widdybank Farm**, crossing the meadows and the rougher pastures beyond. Turn left along a minor road, which some call the **Warden's Road**, and follow it back over the moors, looking out for old mine workings, as well as a brick hut near the top of the road. A gentle descent leads back to the **Cow Green** car park.

WALK 29
Cow Green and Herdship Fell

Distance	16km (10 miles)
Terrain	Fairly easy moorland tracks and paths, but indistinct towards the end.
Start/finish	Cow Green – 810308
Maps	OS Landranger 91; Explorer OL31
Refreshments	None closer than the Langdon Beck Hotel.
Transport	Upper Teesdale buses, operating from Middleton-in-Teesdale and Langdon Beck, except Sundays, will run to Cow Green if booked in advance.

A clear, firm mining track wanders round the western side of Herdship Fell, passing four distinct mining sites. On the Harwood side of the fell, an old road can be combined with vague footpaths to return to Cow Green

The route starts by conveying walkers into the huge, boggy bowl of Upper Teesdale, where there is a great sense of space and wilderness, but then the track suddenly lands on the B6277 on Harwood Common, where the sense of wilderness vanishes like a burst bubble.

The walk around Herdship Fell is pleasant, fairly easy, and likely to be quiet even when the circuit of nearby Widdybank Fell is busy.

Start at the **Cow Green** car park, checking information boards that display basic facts about the geology, scenery, flora and fauna of Upper Teesdale. Follow a track marked as 'No Entry', which only applies to vehicles. Walk along the track, noticing signs of mining straight away. A fine view around Upper Teesdale takes in the sprawling slopes of Mickle Fell, rounded Dun Fells and lofty Cross Fell.

Pass another mining area on **Backside Fell**, drifting away from the head of Cow Green Reservoir. A building on this site has been spared from ruin and serves as a shooting hut. One room is open, if shelter is required in this remote spot.

A shooting hut and a view towards Cross Fell from a mining site on Backside Fell

Continue further along the track to pass another mining area at **Green Hurth**. Follow the track above the ruins, where spoil heaps are infested with rabbits. Walk roughly north along the final part of this track, where mining remains become smaller in scale, and the surrounding moors wilder

and more desolate.
Follow the track as it winds alongside **Crook Burn**, giving the impression that it penetrates even further into the wilderness, although it actually

150

lands suddenly on the **B6277**, one of the highest roads in the country at almost 600m (1970ft).

Turn right along the road, which runs gently downhill. Another right turn reveals the old road to **Harwood**, which drops steeply and gains a tarmac surface when it reaches Frog Hall and **Herdship**. In summer, masses of yellow globe flowers grow on the wet slope between the two farmhouses.

At the next building, which is **Watersmeetings**, turn right to leave the road and walk across fields to reach a ruined chapel beside **Harwood Beck**. Cross a footbridge, then walk downstream to reach a minor road.

Turn right to walk up the road, then right again to reach **Binks House**. Keep left and follow a path climbing indistinctly across the moorland slope. The gradient eases and the path passes some small mine workings. Join a minor road, which some call the **Warden's Road**, at a brick hut. A gentle descent on the road leads back to the car park at **Cow Green**.

WHITEWASH

Dozens of whitewashed farmsteads are dotted throughout Teesdale, and they stand stark against the green fields around Harwood and Langdon Beck. There are many tales to explain the colour scheme. One relates that the Duke of Cleveland was wandering lost on the moors in foul weather. He approached a house for shelter, believing it was occupied by his tenants, and was embarrassed to discover that it wasn't. He ordered all the buildings on his estate to be whitewashed so that he wouldn't make the same mistake again! To this day, Raby Estate properties continue to be whitewashed, with their doorposts and lintels painted black.

SECTION 8
WEARDALE

The low-lying ground in Weardale is excluded from the North Pennines AONB, all the way from Wolsingham, past Stanhope, to Eastgate. The slopes of the dale and the broad and bleak moorlands above are all part of the AONB, including extensive areas primarily managed for grouse shooting. Weardale's mineral wealth has been exploited for centuries and limestone is still extracted above Eastgate. The quarries at Frosterley once produced an intriguing dark, decorative limestone, rich in fossils, known as Frosterley Marble. When the established church was entitled to a tithe on Weardale's mineral wealth, the 'living' at Stanhope was one of the most lucrative in the country.

Five walks explore Weardale, starting with a circuit including Wolsingham and Frosterley, climbing high onto heather moorlands and later returning alongside the River Wear.

An interesting circuit from Stanhope takes in quarries, mines and the surrounding countryside. Westgate is the starting point for a walk that wanders through a former hunting reserve associated with the Bishops of Durham, also visiting the mining village of Rookhope. There is a fine moorland walk high above St John's Chapel and Ireshopeburn. Old railway trackbeds can be followed from Rookhope to Stanhope, featuring steep inclines and the sites of old engine houses. This route can be linked with the Waskerley Way – see Walk 35.

Stanhope is the main population centre in Weardale, and offers a full range of services and facilities. The Durham Dales Centre is based there, offering plenty of information about the North Pennines. The North Pennines AONB office is also located in town, producing a fine range of publications, as well as promoting events.

WALK 30

Wolsingham and Frosterley

Distance	16km (10 miles)
Terrain	Mostly easy field paths, moorland tracks and minor roads.
Start/finish	Market Place, Wolsingham – 076373
Maps	OS Landranger 92; Explorer OL31
Refreshments	Pubs at Wolsingham and Frosterley.
Transport	Regular daily Weardale buses serve Wolsingham and Frosterley from Bishop Auckland and Stanhope, along with occasional rail services.

The Weardale Way is usually a low-level walk, but between Wolsingham and Frosterley it climbs high onto heathery moorlands. The so-called Elephant Trees stand high on the moorland edge and are a landmark from all points around Weardale. A moorland track proves popular with walkers and cyclists, being broad and firm enough to accommodate both. Walkers can use riverside footpaths to return from Frosterley to Wolsingham, parallel to the Weardale Railway.

The villages of Frosterley and Wolsingham are designated conservation areas. Frosterley's old quarries once produced decorative, fossil-rich Frosterley Marble, which took a high polish and was much sought for monumental work. A town trail around Wolsingham could be enjoyed before or after this walk.

WOLSINGHAM

Wolsingham is a designated conservation area and a town trail reveals a wealth of interesting old buildings. Of particular note near the start of this walk are the Whitfield Cottages, formerly the Pack Horse Inn, bearing an old date-stone in Roman numerals that translates as 1677. Wolsingham was already an established market town in the dale, but in 1864 it also became an industrial centre when it acquired a steelworks. The parish church of St Mary and St Stephen lies in a quiet quarter of the town seldom explored by visitors.

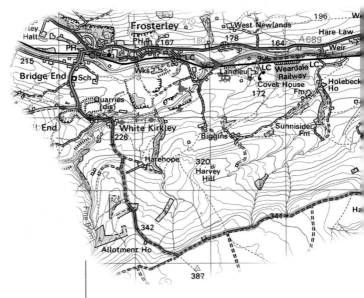

Leave the market place in **Wolsingham** as if going along the A689 to Stanhope, but turn left along a minor road signposted for Hamsterley. A bridge spans the **River Wear** and another bridge spans the railway, then the road climbs steeply uphill. Avoid a bend by taking the course of an old road, now a path, on the left.

Just before rejoining the road, cross a ladder-stile on the left, then climb straight up through fields, watching for stiles and gates to reach **Chatterley Farm**. Turn right along the access track, then left uphill by road.

Pass the access road for **Rushy Lea**, then keep bearing right along roads and tracks, until the narrow road becomes a gravel track running beside moors high above Weardale.

Don't follow the track heading left to the isolated farm of **Harthope**, but go straight onwards through a gate to get onto the heather moorlands. A clear track is generally surfaced with sand or gravel and it never strays too far

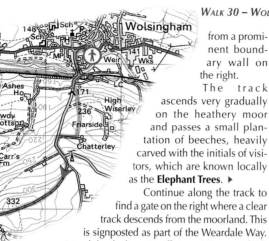

from a prominent boundary wall on the right.

The track ascends very gradually on the heathery moor and passes a small plantation of beeches, heavily carved with the initials of visitors, which are known locally as the **Elephant Trees**. ▸

Continue along the track to find a gate on the right where a clear track descends from the moorland. This is signposted as part of the Weardale Way. A track leads down to **Allotment House**, which is a large barn. A narrow tarmac road continues downhill, passing odd stands of trees.

The road leads through the tiny hamlet of **White Kirkley**, then climbs up to a road junction, passing old quarries on the way. Turn right at the junction and walk downhill again, passing a school and crossing a bridge over the **River Wear** and railway to reach **Frosterley** via the Black Bull Inn.

Only you can decide whether they really look like elephants marching across the skyline when seen on the horizon from different parts of Weardale.

FROSTERLEY MARBLE

This 'marble' is actually a dark and durable limestone that can be cut and polished in the same way as true marble. Unlike marble, the stone contains fossils, particularly solitary corals, which create bizarre and intriguing forms when seen in cross section. Look out for Frosterley Marble when visiting notable buildings in the area, and examples can also be seen by making a detour into interesting Harehope Quarry near Frosterley, tel 01388 528599, www.harehopequarry.org.

As soon as the main A689 is reached at **Frosterley**, turn right and walk along a narrow footpath. This leads round the back of the village, passing the parish church and wandering along a patchy tarmac road. Keep right to follow this road gradually down past Mill Cottages to a railway line.

Don't cross the railway line, but turn left to follow a footpath and another road. Before reaching the main road, watch for a path squeezing past the left side of a row of houses. This leads close to a bridge over the **River Wear**.

Don't cross the railway line, but turn left and follow a path that runs between the River Wear and the railway. At first there is no access to the river, then a riverside path can be followed.

When a **caravan site** is reached, follow its access road away to the next bridge. Don't cross the bridge, but continue straight onwards to follow a field path running parallel to a railway line.

Eventually, a flight of steps leads up to a bridge near a railway station. Turn left to cross the bridge over the **River Wear**, then right to follow a riverside path through a caravan site to return to the market place in the centre of **Wolsingham**.

The Weardale Railway has a station just outside Wolsingham

WEARDALE RAILWAY

A line was constructed in 1847, by the Stockton & Darlington Railway Company, running from Bishop Auckland into Weardale, reaching Wearhead by 1895. Limestone was transported along the line to Teesside ironworks. A passenger service ceased in 1953, though freight continued from the cement works at Eastgate until 1993. The Weardale Railway Preservation Society was formed and trains now run between Wolsingham and Stanhope, though there is a long-term plan to offer services all the way from Bishop Auckland to Eastgate. Tel 0845 6001348, www.weardale-railway.org.uk.

WALK 31
Stanhope and Stanhope Dene

Distance	8km (5 miles)
Terrain	Mostly easy field paths and moorland tracks, but occasionally pathless with some steep slopes.
Start/finish	Durham Dales Centre, Stanhope – 996392
Maps	OS Landrangers 87 and 92; Explorer 307
Refreshments	Pubs at Stanhope.
Transport	Regular daily Weardale buses serve Stanhope from Wearhead and Bishop Auckland.

Fine countryside lies north of Stanhope, where little fields quickly give way to quarried slopes, followed by open moorland. This walk climbs to Crawleyside by way of a quarried edge now reverting to nature. An old railway incline leads onto open moorlands, then the pleasant Velvet Path runs down to a mining site in Stanhope Dene. Another climb leads to the fringes of extensive moorland, where the route runs easily alongside a forest. A final descent leads back down through fields to Stanhope Dene and so back to Stanhope. Plenty of background information about this part of the North Pennines can be obtained from the Durham Dales Centre.

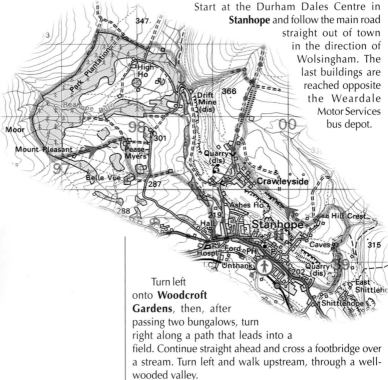

Start at the Durham Dales Centre in **Stanhope** and follow the main road straight out of town in the direction of Wolsingham. The last buildings are reached opposite the Weardale Motor Services bus depot.

Turn left onto **Woodcroft Gardens**, then, after passing two bungalows, turn right along a path that leads into a field. Continue straight ahead and cross a footbridge over a stream. Turn left and walk upstream, through a well-wooded valley.

The path climbs above the flow then drops down stone steps to cross another footbridge. Climb stone steps on the other side and, partway up them, turn right along a narrow path and head further up through the wooded valley. Emerge from the woods to ford the stream, then follow a wall that runs parallel to the stream, fording it again at a stand of trees.

Climb uphill and pass above a few buildings at **Hill Crest** to reach a track. Cross the track and head straight across heather to reach another track, then turn right to follow it.

There are walls on either side of the track, and on the left the wall heads downhill, while on the right the wall heads uphill. Follow neither, but watch for a path in between, traversing Crawley Edge on the fringe of a moor, overlooking buildings at **Crawleyside**.

The path approaches a road, but there is no need to walk on tarmac. Stay on the moor to pass the last building, then pick up a cinder-strewn track. This was formerly a railway incline, which used to carry waggons between the Weatherhill Engine and the Crawley Engine. Climb the incline, parallel to the road, passing a rectangular walled enclosure.

Afterwards, turn left to cross the **B6278**. A footpath sign reveals a track running down and round a moorland valley, passing a metal memorial bench. Part of this track is known as the **Velvet Path**, being covered in short green turf. The final descent is stony and leads down through a gate to some derelict mining buildings in **Stanhope Dene**.

Turn right to follow a track to a bridge over **Stanhope Burn**. Don't cross the stream, but follow a narrow and crumbling path upstream. Later, the stream needs to be forded to reach a stile, which would be awkward after heavy rain. Walk up through a field and keep to the left of **Hope House**, expecting to be greeted by some of the dogs from the Animal Rescue that is based there.

Follow the access track away from the building, but don't enter the forest of **Park Plantation**. Instead, turn right to follow a track uphill alongside the forest. When the track pulls away from the trees, continue alongside the boundary wall to reach the top corner of the forest on the fringe of **Stanhope Common**.

Turn left to pick up and follow a track running beside **Park Plantation**, which diminishes on the grassy moorland. Pass a crater-like quarry and cross **Reahope Burn**. Climb uphill alongside the forest then descend slightly on **Reahope Moor**, with a view into Weardale. Turn left through a gate, passing through a narrow part of the forest, then pass **Mount Pleasant.** Walk down an access track to reach another farm at **Pease Myers**.

Stanhope Burn needs to be forded to reach a stile

Don't go down the access track, but turn right up through the farmyard then left through a gate into a field. Walk straight ahead to spot a gate, then a stile, then head towards a house, turning left to go through a small gate as marked. Continue down through a field and cross a road.

Walk down an access track to reach a house at **Widley Field**. There are two gates, so go through the one on the right and cross a field diagonally. Cross a stile in the far corner then turn left to cross another stile and enter a wood.

Walk a short way to join a path in **Stanhope Dene** and turn right. The path leads to a main road near **Stanhope Hall**, where a left turn leads straight back into **Stanhope.**

STANHOPE

Stanhope is a designated conservation area, and the parish church of St Thomas, with its 'fossil tree', dominates the market place. The 'living' of this parish was once one of the wealthiest in the country. Rectors were entitled to a tithe of one-tenth on all the lead mined in Weardale, and could afford to live elsewhere in grand style, employing lowly curates to do their work. This was resented by most of the dalesfolk, especially those engaged in lead mining, and the spread of Nonconformism created plenty of local friction with the established church. The tithe was abolished in the 19th century.

Stanhope Castle lies behind a wall, and few visitors are aware of its presence. It was constructed in 1798 and bankrupted the builder. A group of miners who were caught poaching grouse were locked up at the Bonny Moor Hen pub on their way to Durham gaol. Their comrades stormed the building, beating the keepers and constables who were on guard, and rescued the inmates. The event is commemorated in verse, and no one was ever brought to trial. Stanhope has a full range of facilities, and the Durham Dales Centre houses a tourist information centre, tel 01388 527650, www.durhamdalescentre.co.uk.

WALK 32
Westgate, Middlehope and Rookhope

Distance	16km (10 miles)
Terrain	Easy field paths and tracks, but rough and vague moorland paths.
Start/finish	Westgate – 907381
Maps	OS Landrangers 87 and 92; OL31 and 307
Refreshments	Pubs at Westgate and Rookhope.
Transport	Regular daily Weardale buses serve Westgate from Stanhope and Wearhead. Occasional weekday Weardale buses serve Rookhope from Stanhope.

Westgate, Eastgate and Northgate are placenames in this part of Weardale – but there is no Southgate. The 'gates' marked the boundary of an ancient hunting forest frequented by the Bishops of Durham. The foundations of their hunting lodge can be seen near the road between Eastgate and Westgate.

The following walk wanders through this ancient preserve, but concentrates more on mining and quarrying activities. The route climbs from Westgate over to Rookhope, returning by way of Northgate Fell. The ascent via Middlehope Burn reveals a delightfully overgrown lead-mining site, softened by nature, with waterfalls splashing alongside. After walking across moors around Hangingwells Common to reach Rookhope, an old railway trackbed can be followed back round Northgate Fell to return to Westgate.

Follow the Rookhope road out of **Westgate**, which bends to the right where a short track heads off to the left. Follow this track, then walk upstream beside **Middlehope Burn**, passing an old mill and a couple of lovely waterfalls.

The narrow track is well wooded and leads to a more open area, passing the arches of a former bousesteads, where untreated ore, or 'bouse', was stored. The river has been enclosed in stone-built tunnels and it is quite possible to walk over its course without even realising. However, stay on the eastern bank of the river to continue upstream along a path.

After passing a small waterfall, another lead-mining site is reached, and the dark mouth of a level can be seen off to the right. Further upstream, the entrance arch to another level has a gate across it. A track crosses the path at this point, and by turning right, it can be followed up to another track.

Turn left along this track and follow it up to a minor road. Turn right along the road to reach **Scarsike Head**, which is a moorland gap. Don't cross the gap, but turn right down another road, as if going back to Westgate.

Follow the road until a prominent track runs off to the left, flanked by walls. Walk along the track and go through a gate at the end of it. Head straight across the moors of **Hangingwells Common**, and try not to be confused by the number of

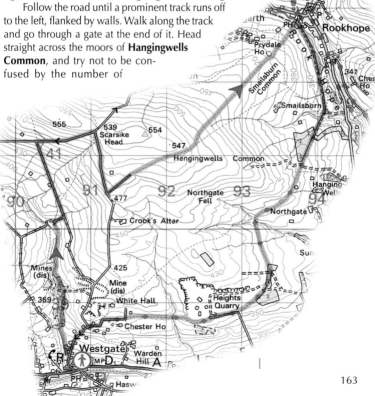

vague paths trodden on the ground. Don't worry too much about straying off-course, as either a stone wall or a wire fence will be reached before too long.

If the wall is reached, turn right, but if the fence is reached, turn left. A gateway stands where the wall and fence meet. Technically, the right of way crosses a stile nearby over the fence, though there is no trodden path to or from it. Either go through the gate, or cross the stile over the fence, then use the course of the stone wall running downhill to the northeast as a guide across **Smailsburn Common**.

The village of Rookhope will be seen ahead, and a small reservoir is passed before the final part of the descent. When a clear track is reached, there is an option to head into **Rookhope**, which has a shop and pub, returning to this point later.

Old railway trackbeds and the remnants of industrial heritage are found around Rookhope

To continue the walk without visiting the village, turn right to follow the track, which accompanies **Rookhope Burn** downstream. The track follows the course of an old railway trackbed, climbing gently up past a small forest to reach a farm at **Smailsburn**. After passing the farm,

a steeper stretch of the trackbed leads through another small forest, then the old line begins to level out as it crosses **Northgate Fell**.

The trackbed bends to the right and runs towards a prominent embankment, where it bends to the left and runs through a cutting. Emerge from the cutting and cross quarry spoil to join the access road from **Heights Quarry**. Cross the road then pass the quarry as marked to continue along the trackbed.

A viaduct once spanned **Park Burn**, but has been demolished, so walkers must descend to cross the stream, then climb. Further along, the trackbed has to be abandoned, so turn left, then right to join and follow a farm access road.

The farm access road leads down to a minor road that is itself followed steeply down to **Westgate**. The railway trackbed from Rookhope ended with a steep descent to Westgate, with waggons hauled up and down by a winding engine.

THE HUNTING LODGE

Part of this walk runs within an ancient hunting preserve. The Bishops of Durham had a hunting lodge in Weardale from 1430, and its square platform site can be seen beside the road between Eastgate and Westgate. Such activities were frowned upon after the Reformation and hunting ceased. In earlier centuries, the Romans hunted in Weardale. Caius Testius Micianus captured a huge boar that no one else had managed to take, and erected an altar to Silvanus, the god of the hunt. A replica can be seen beside the road at Eastgate, and is one of many altars dedicated to Silvanus in this area. Travelling further back in time, the bones of exotic creatures long extinct in this country have been discovered in caves in Weardale, and it seems fair to assume that the earliest settlers also enjoyed the thrill of the chase.

WALK 33
Chapelfell Top and Noon Hill

Distance	11km (7 miles)
Terrain	Good tracks and paths on the lower slopes, but also rugged, exposed, pathless moorland.
Start/finish	St John's Chapel – 885379
Maps	OS Landrangers 91 or 92; Explorer OL31
Refreshments	Pubs at St John's Chapel and Ireshopeburn.
Transport	Regular daily Weardale buses serve St John's Chapel and Ireshopeburn from Bishop Auckland and Stanhope.

Wesley preached at Ireshopeburn between 1750 and 1790. He had a high regard for Pennine dalesfolk and Methodist chapels are abundant throughout the area. Trekking over from Teesdale, Wesley noted that 'from the top of an enormous mountain we had a view of Weardale. It is a lovely prospect; the green, gently rising meadows and fields, on both sides of the little river as clear as crystal, were sprinkled all over with innumerable little houses'. Surely the 'enormous mountain' was Chapelfell Top, and this route features a stone in the shape of a chair that offers just such a prospect.

Rights of way lead from Weardale towards Chapelfell Top and Noon Hill, but expire on the moorland slopes. However, the moors feature designated open access land and a link between the two summits uses a fence as a guide.

A small church is dedicated to St John in the village of **St John's Chapel**. A bridleway sign nearby points across the road and reveals a track behind the Golden Lion pub. This grassy track is easy to follow as it zigzags uphill, and wet patches alongside are rich in orchids. Pass the restored farmhouse of **Thatch Mires** and keep climbing.

When another track is reached, turn right to continue uphill, noting mountain pansies in early summer. A gate at the end of the track leads onto open moorland where a large container serves as a storage shed. The public bridleway expires near here, but the high moorlands feature

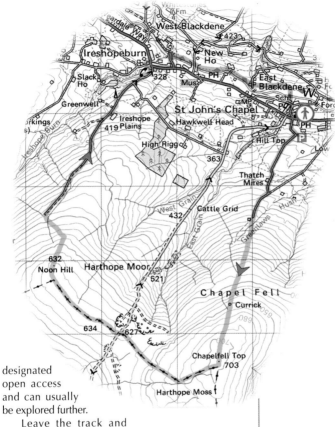

designated
open access
and can usually
be explored further.

   Leave the track and
aim for the corner of a wall seen on the skyline. The
gradient eases above the wall, then steepens again,
and it is possible that a boulder in the shape of a crude
chair might be noticed in passing. Only a small cairn
stands on the broad, peaty summit of **Chapelfell Top** at
703m (2306ft). There are views beyond Weardale and
Teesdale, but the sprawling moorland slopes obscure
the dale bottoms.

167

A small cairn sits near a junction of fences on the moorland top of Noon Hill

Keep walking across the peat hags and groughs to reach a wire fence, and look out for cloudberry growing among the heather and bilberry. Turn right to follow the fence across the moors, wandering away from it to find the best way through the hags and groughs, aiming to reach a minor road at a cattle-grid at **Harthope Cross**.

The road runs at an altitude of 627m (2056ft) and is one of the highest roads in the country. Cross over it and continue following the fence, passing above an old 'ganister' quarry where tiered beds of hard sandstone can be seen. There is hardly any ascent worth mentioning as the fence continues to **Noon Hill**.

Fences meet on the grassy summit and the route passes through a gateway. Turn right to follow a fence down to a wall, then turn left to follow the wall to an old railway carriage that now serves as a storage shed.

A clear, walled track is another public bridleway, giving a direct descent from the moors. Follow the track downhill, and it later becomes a tarmac road leading into the village of **Ireshopeburn**. Turn right along the **A689** and follow it to the Weardale Museum of **High House Chapel**, where the adjacent Weardale Inn offers food and drink. Either visit one or the other, or continue the walk by following a minor road across the **River Wear**.

WEARDALE MUSEUM

High House Chapel was built in 1760 and claims to be the second oldest Methodist chapel still in use. The Weardale Museum of High House Chapel is in the former minister's house. Exhibits celebrate the life, work and history of Weardale, and one room is devoted to Wesley, who preached to the dalesfolk from a corner on the road outside, where a memorial now stands. The museum was established as a local venture, winning a Carnegie 'Interpret Britain' award. The trackbed of the Weardale Extension Railway passes between the museum and the River Wear and was constructed in 1895. Unfortunately it came too late for the lead-mining industry, which was already in terminal decline. Tel 01388 517433, www.weardalemuseum.co.uk.

After crossing the **River Wear**, turn right along a riverside path, which is part of the Weardale Way. Follow the path past two footbridges, maybe making a slight detour to visit a fine waterfall, then cross over another footbridge further downstream. A path leads to a road, which in turn leads to the main road in the middle of **St John's Chapel**.

It is worth making a short detour to see a small waterfall on the way back to St John's Chapel

WALK 34
Rookhope to Stanhope

Distance	13km (8 miles)
Terrain	A high-level moorland track with some steep gradients at the start and finish.
Start	Rookhope – 939429
Finish	Stanhope – 996392
Maps	OS Landrangers 87 and 92; Explorer 307
Refreshments	Pub at Rookhope. Café at Parkhead. Plenty of choice around Stanhope.
Transport	Occasional weekday Weardale buses serve Rookhope from Stanhope. Regular daily Weardale buses serve Stanhope from Bishop Auckland.

This linear walk makes use of old railway trackbeds running across moorlands as high as 500m (1640ft), as well as going up and down steep inclines that connected them with settlements in Weardale.

There are actually two railway lines – one from Rookhope to Parkhead and the other from Parkhead to Stanhope. They were constructed to serve mines and quarries, and because of their inclines, they were unsuitable for passenger transport. However, there was a brief period when passenger trains from Consett ran to Parkhead Station, which now offers food, drink and accommodation in a remote area.

Leave **Rookhope** at a road bend between the Rookhope Inn and post office shop. Blue cycleway markers indicate National Route 7 – a popular coast-to-coast cycleway known as the C2C.

Climb straight uphill to leave the village and pass through a gate to walk up an old railway trackbed. Pass a battered tin hut and follow the stony incline high onto the moors. The track passes through a cutting where a ruined stone building housed a winding engine.

REDGATE HEAD WINDING ENGINE

Around 1845 the Weardale Iron Company asked the Stockton & Darlington Railway to extend their line from Parkhead to Rookhope, but they were obliged to build it at their own expense. Trucks were hauled up from Rookhope by a static engine then hitched to a steam locomotive to be hauled across the moors to Consett. Closure came piecemeal over the years. The last thing seen on the branch line above Rookhope was a battery-powered car, taking grouse shooters in search of sport in 1925. The track was lifted in 1943.

An old boiler lies marooned and rusting beside a sheepfold beyond Redgate Head

The old trackbed runs level and easy around 510m (1675ft) across the heathery slopes of **Bolt's Law**. The only feature of note lies off to the right, where a large rusting boiler sits incongruously beside a sheepfold.

Soon afterwards, there may be a glimpse across a moorland gap at **Dead Friars** of the distant city of Newcastle. Keep straight ahead at a junction, avoiding a track rising gently to the left, which leads off-route.

The old trackbed proceeds broad and grassy, with a narrow cinder strip that is favoured by cyclists. Later, an embankment has a boggy strip to the left, while a cinder slope falls to the right.

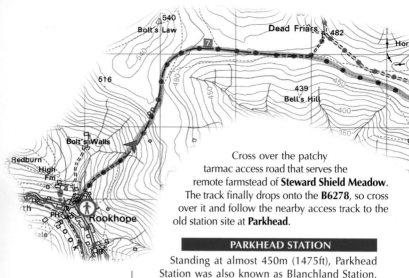

Cross over the patchy tarmac access road that serves the remote farmstead of **Steward Shield Meadow**. The track finally drops onto the **B6278**, so cross over it and follow the nearby access track to the old station site at **Parkhead**.

PARKHEAD STATION

Standing at almost 450m (1475ft), Parkhead Station was also known as Blanchland Station, despite being 10km (6 miles) away from the village. It was an important junction, where trucks laden with limestone from Stanhope met other trucks laden with ore from Rookhope, all to be hauled across the moors to Consett. The sand quarry near Parkhead ensured that the line remained open at this point until 1968, before being closed for good. The old station site now offers accommodation and a café, proving popular with C2C cyclists, who continue their cross-country journey along the Waskerley Way (see Walk 35).

On reaching **Parkhead**, turn right to follow a clear, firm, level cinder track away from a car park towards a rusty corrugated building in the distance. Keep well to the right of this building, which is on the site of the old **Weatherhill Engine**, then walk down an incline covered in short green turf. This part of the railway was closed in 1951.

Drop downhill parallel to the **B6278** and pass through a gentle heathery cutting. Continue along a low, cinder embankment that is being undermined by rabbit burrows. Buildings are reached at **Crawleyside**, the site of the former Crawley Engine.

Either keep left of the buildings on a right of way, or keep right of them by road. If keeping left, later turn left along a grassy path. If keeping right, wait until the road begins to drop steeply, then go through a gate on the left, signposted as a public footpath, and follow a grassy path.

The path runs beside a fence and a wall, rising gently along a heathery brow overlooking Crawleyside and Stanhope. Between the two settlements is a long, grassy embankment of quarry spoil. Watch carefully for a footpath marker indicating a narrow path veering down to the right through heather and bracken. It runs beside a fence and goes through two kissing gates.

Walk beside a huge **quarry**, aiming for two metal footbridges spanning a narrow part. Walk straight down into **Stanhope**, turning left along a road to pass the Methodist church, then right down a narrow road beside the parish church to reach the centre of town.

SECTION 9
DERWENTSIDE

The northeastern part of the North Pennines is drained by the River Derwent, which is a tributary of the mighty River Tyne. The upper reaches of the river have been dammed to form the Derwent Reservoir, which is seen by anyone travelling to and fro between Edmundbyers and Blanchland. The largest settlement in this area lies just outside the North Pennines AONB. Consett is a former steelworks town struggling to find itself a modern identity, though it could be regarded as a natural 'gateway' to the North Pennines. The town is well known among cyclists following the C2C, a coast-to-coast cycleway.

Three walks are described around Derwentside. The first is the Waskerley Way, which is an integral part of the C2C cycleway, and therefore open to cyclists as well as walkers. It makes use of an old railway trackbed, linking with other old trackbeds running

at remarkable heights across grouse-shooting moorlands. At Edmundbyers a stretch of the Lead Mining Trail can be followed from lowland pastures onto open moorlands, returning to the village afterwards. Blanchland is a remarkable village, constructed from the ruins of an ancient abbey, where much of the original ground plan is easily recognised in the current plan of the village. It is easy to become distracted and forget to go walking, but a fine circuit runs round the heather moorlands of Blanchland Common and back to the village.

Consett has the most services in this area, and is the natural hub for public transport. Since the demise of its many railway lines, the town is now served by buses, many of them heading to and from Newcastle, but some visiting nearby villages. Outside Consett, facilities in the villages are rather limited, but there are pubs and accommodation.

WALK 35
Waskerley Way – Parkhead to Consett

Distance	17km (10½ miles)
Terrain	A high-level moorland track giving way to cultivated countryside.
Start	Parkhead Station – 003431
Finish	Consett – 107508
Maps	OS Landrangers 87 and 88; Explorer 307
Refreshments	Café at Parkhead. Plenty of choice around Consett.
Transport	None to Parkhead. Regular daily Go North East buses serve Consett from Newcastle.

The Waskerley Way is the name given to an old railway trackbed between Parkhead and Consett that has been converted for walking and cycling. It is an essential link in National Route 7 – a coast-to-coast cycleway known as the C2C. The Stanhope & Tyne Railway opened in 1834 and was a peculiar line, with level stretches broken by severe gradients. Horsepower operated on the level parts, while static winding engines hauled trucks up and down the steep inclines. After being taken over and overhauled in the 1840s by the Stockton & Darlington Railway, the line operated until its final closure in 1969.

There is no public transport to Parkhead Station, so arrange to be dropped at that point, then spend the rest of the day walking this linear route to Consett, which has bus services.

PARKHEAD STATION

Standing at almost 450m (1475ft), Parkhead Station was also known as Blanchland Station, despite being 10km (6 miles) away from the village. It was an important junction, where trucks laden with lime-stone from Stanhope met other trucks laden with ore from Rookhope, all to be hauled across the moors to Consett. The sand quarry near Parkhead ensured that the line remained open at this point until 1968,

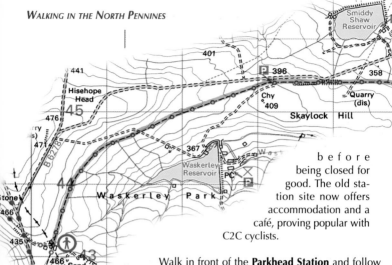

before being closed for good. The old station site now offers accommodation and a café, proving popular with C2C cyclists.

map continued on page 178

Walk in front of the **Parkhead Station** and follow the level railway trackbed through a gate onto the open heather moorlands of **Waskerley Park**. Pass a barrier and cross a grassy track. The grassy track could be used to visit Waskerley Reservoir as a detour. Pass a gate and another barrier to reach a car park below an old chimney on **Skaylock Hill**, where an access road climbs from Waskerley Reservoir.

Head gently downhill along the track, which runs parallel to a minor road and overlooks **Smiddy Shaw Reservoir**. Go through a gate to pass the railway hamlet of **Waskerley**, where only a few buildings remain, including an old engine shed.

Go through a gate into a forest, then climb gently towards **Burnhill Junction**, where a sharp left turn is made onto another old trackbed beside a securely fenced old MOD site. (Before reaching the junction, there is an option to short-cut from a gate on the left, directly through rushy fields to Red House. Closer to the junction, a lesser short-cut links the two old trackbeds.)

Instead of passing through a boggy, wooded cutting, use spur paths to the right and left, climbing above the cutting before passing **Red House**. (Bee Cottage

Farmhouse bed and breakfast lies just off-route.)

Head downhill along an embankment and pick up the course of the old trackbed again. Further along, a bridge spans the route, while later a minor road is crossed at **Whitehall**.

The busy A68 is crossed at **Rowley**, close to a Baptist church dated 1652. A railway station was removed stone by stone from this point and rebuilt at the North of England Museum at Beamish. Continue past a farm and its access road at **Middle Heads** then cross over lofty **Hownes Gill Viaduct**. To see it to its best advantage, it really needs to be viewed from below.

HOWNES GILL VIADUCT

When the Stanhope & Tyne Railway opened in 1834, the gradients at Hownes Gill were most severe, being 1 in 3. The company went bankrupt in 1840, partly due to inefficiencies on inclines such as Hownes Gill. The Stockton & Darlington Railway Company took over the line and constructed the Hownes Gill Viaduct in 1858. This consumed 2.5 million bricks and rose to a height of 50m (150ft). The railway finally closed in 1969.

One of the strange 'Terris Novalis' sculptures on the way into Consett

177

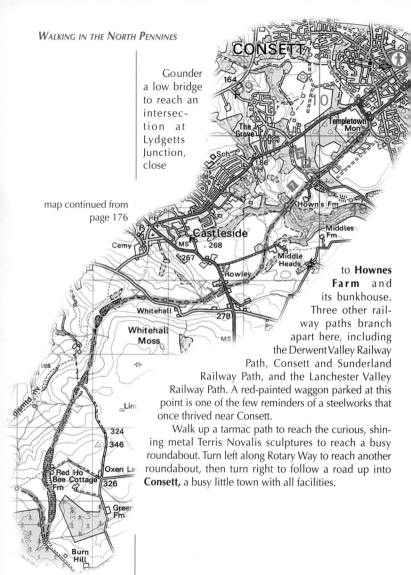

Go under a low bridge to reach an intersection at Lydgetts Junction, close

map continued from page 176

to **Hownes Farm** and its bunkhouse. Three other railway paths branch apart here, including the Derwent Valley Railway Path, Consett and Sunderland Railway Path, and the Lanchester Valley Railway Path. A red-painted waggon parked at this point is one of the few reminders of a steelworks that once thrived near Consett.

Walk up a tarmac path to reach the curious, shining metal Terris Novalis sculptures to reach a busy roundabout. Turn left along Rotary Way to reach another roundabout, then turn right to follow a road up into **Consett,** a busy little town with all facilities.

WALK 36

Edmundbyers and Edmundbyers Common

Distance	14km (9 miles)
Terrain	Mostly easy tracks and paths up through fields, then back across exposed moorlands.
Start/finish	Edmundbyers – 017501
Maps	OS Landranger 87; Explorer 307
Refreshments	Pub at Edmundbyers.
Transport	Occasional Weardale buses serve Edmundbyers from Consett on weekdays.

Edmundbyers is a quiet little Derwentside village arranged around a large green. The walk starts close to the parish church of St Edmund, and follows tracks and paths up through pleasant meadows and pastures, passing derelict farmsteads to reach heather moorland above the Ramshaw valley. The return to Edmundbyers takes a parallel course, but is almost entirely across moorland and so presents quite a different aspect.

The route described is also a loop on the Lead Mining Trail, which stretches all the way from Cowshill, at the head of Weardale, over to Edmundbyers. Lead mining becomes more apparent on the upper part of this particular walk, where the chimneys of old mines come into view in the Ramshaw valley.

Follow the B6278 out of **Edmundbyers** in the direction of Stanhope. Pass St Edmund's Church and head downhill towards a bridge, but do not cross it. Instead, turn right at a sharp bend before the bridge and follow a track. Don't follow this track up to a farm, but turn left along another track across a slope of gorse and bracken, roughly parallel to **Burnhope Burn**.

A good track is reached later, where a right turn leads up past the old farmstead of **College**. The track continues rising gently to go through another farmyard at **Pedam's Oak**. Apparently there was once a hollow oak tree here, and a horse thief named Pedam hid inside it to avoid being caught.

The track descends slightly, then climbs up through fields again to pass the old farmstead of **Belmount**. Keep above this site to follow a track, which in turn follows a wall gently up onto open moorland.

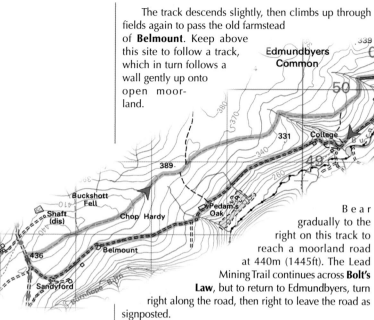

B e a r gradually to the right on this track to reach a moorland road at 440m (1445ft). The Lead Mining Trail continues across **Bolt's Law**, but to return to Edmundbyers, turn right along the road, then right to leave the road as signposted.

The way across the moorland is vague at first, but soon a left turn leads along a clear track. Later, leave the track by turning right to reach a line of grouse-shooting butts near a gate. Go through the gate and continue walking gently downhill following the broadest track across the moor.

Another gate at **Chop Hardy** marks a transition from heather moorland to predominantly grassy moorland, but the track passes back onto heather moorland at another gate.

Continue to trace the broad and grassy track across the moors, still descending gradually. There is a bend in the track where it passes grouse-shooting butts and crosses a stream, then the route runs below an isolated field system on **Edmundbyers Common**. After crossing another stream the track joins a road and a short descent leads back into **Edmundbyers**.

EDMUNDBYERS

Edmundbyers is a quiet little village with no facilities beyond a pub and youth hostel. The hostel was once a pub called the Low House Inn. It stood at a strategic point on packhorse ways, catching passing trade from Tynedale, Allendale and Weardale. It is reputed to be haunted by the ghost of a former landlord who died of exposure while searching the moors for his wife, who had gone missing. St Edmund's Church has a little Saxon and Norman stonework incorporated into its more recently 'restored' fabric. The altar-stone is unusual,

A series of stone water troughs can be seen on one of the greens in Edmundbyers

being made of a single slab of stone in a type forbidden following the Reformation. The slab was removed, but wasn't destroyed. It was buried in the churchyard, where it was rediscovered in 1855, and has since been restored to its original position in the church.

WALK 37
Blanchland and Blanchland Moor

Distance	14km (8¾ miles)
Terrain	A fine moorland track leads to a forest, then a more difficult moorland path leads to a road and gentle riverside walking.
Start/finish	Blanchland – 965503
Maps	OS Landranger 87; Explorer OL43
Refreshments	Pub and tea room in Blanchland.
Transport	Occasional Weardale buses serve Blanchland from Consett on weekdays.

Blanchland is beautiful – a term seldom used for North Pennine settlements, which are often rather stern and utilitarian. Blanchland is inseparable from its Premonstratensian abbey, portions of which are found all around the village.

There are lead mines in the area, and the paths and tracks used on this walk were once frequented by miners heading to and from work. Today, Blanchland Moor is a broad expanse of heather, managed for grouse shooting, and while the outward track is clear and obvious, the Carrier's Way used for the return needs a bit more care to locate.

BLANCHLAND

Blanchland is dominated by the ample remains of its Premonstratensian abbey, which was founded in 1165. The term 'blanch' refers to the white habits worn by the monks, and the placename Blanchland was recorded as early as 1214. In the 14th century the abbey was crowned with a fine tower. After the Dissolution the property passed to the Radcliffe family, then to the Forster family, during which time the stonework was plundered so much that the only place of worship was a small chapel situated near the abbey entrance. In 1699 Lord Crewe, Bishop of Durham, married into the Forster family and came to hold the property. He died in 1721, leaving it in the care of trustees, who built the present Abbey Church by filling in gaps between the ruined choir, leaving it with an L-shaped ground plan. Several items of stonework are preserved in the church, which is as good as a museum and well worth a visit.

The village of Blanchland is based on the plan of the Abbey outbuildings. The large gatehouse is now a post office shop. The abbot's lodge, or guest house, is now the Lord Crewe Arms. Inside the building a vaulted chamber serves as a bar, one fireplace is big enough for people to dine inside, and the gardens outside are based on the abbey cloister and chapter house. The large gravel courtyard in the village is surrounded by restored cottages that were once the refectory, dormitories and workshops of the monks and lay brethren.

Start by exploring the village of **Blanchland**, then head for the main car park as signposted. Just before reaching it, turn right to find a grassy track climbing uphill from a

The village of Blanchland is largely based on the ground plan of a Premonstratensian abbey

183

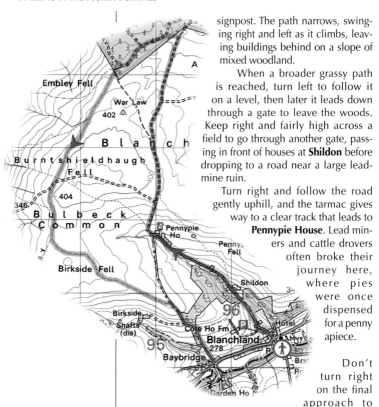

signpost. The path narrows, swinging right and left as it climbs, leaving buildings behind on a slope of mixed woodland.

When a broader grassy path is reached, turn left to follow it on a level, then later it leads down through a gate to leave the woods. Keep right and fairly high across a field to go through another gate, passing in front of houses at **Shildon** before dropping to a road near a large lead-mine ruin.

Turn right and follow the road gently uphill, and the tarmac gives way to a clear track that leads to **Pennypie House**. Lead miners and cattle drovers often broke their journey here, where pies were once dispensed for a penny apiece.

Don't turn right on the final approach to the house, but go straight ahead through a gate onto a moor instead. Turn right to follow a track uphill beside a wall and go through a gate on top to reach open heather moorland. Follow the clear track straight ahead across **Blanchland Moor**, with the Cheviot Hills seen in the far distance.

Go through another gate not far below the summit of **War Law** and follow the track gently down towards a forest. Watch out for a sharp left turn revealing a path leading up to a forest gate. Enter the forest and follow one track to another track and turn left. Walk through a clear-felled part of the forest and turn left again to follow a track to a gate in the forest fence.

Go through the gate, but don't follow the path straight ahead, along a stony groove through the heather on **Embley Fell**. Instead, bear half-left along a less distinct heathery groove, looking ahead to spot what looks like a line of stone cairns – actually a line of shooting butts alongside the groove. There is a path of sorts, and in time it gets a little better, leading to a gate in a fence.

Go through the gate and continue along the groove, or if it is wet, use a path alongside. This rises gently across the heather moors of **Burntshieldhaugh Fell**, overlooking the valley of Devil's Water, with Allendale Common and Killhope Law in view.

Pass intersections with other paths and tracks, always walking straight ahead. A hut will be noticed down to the right, and later the path goes through a gate in a drystone wall in a slight dip.

When a waymarked path junction is reached on **Bulbeck Common**, veer left along another bridleway, which is a grassy path over the heather moorland of **Birkside Fell**. Go through a gate in a fence and follow a firm track gently down the moorland slope, later running parallel to a drystone wall.

Go through another gate in a fence and continue through a field, still parallel to the wall. Go through a gate at the far end of the field, keep left of a gas pipeline installation, then follow its access road down through a gate.

The road drops steeply beside a plantation of Scots pines on a slope of crumbling shale. Follow the road all the way down to the little village of **Baybridge**, and go straight ahead towards the **River Derwent**.

Either turn left to follow a riverside path through fields, or cross a bridge over the river and turn left to follow a path across a wooded slope. Both options lead back to **Blanchland**, where any spare time can be enjoyed exploring the place again.

SECTION 10
DEVIL'S WATER

Devil's Water drains a verdant valley that is squeezed between Derwentside and Allendale, yet belongs to neither. Although of limited extent, and served by a tortuous system of dead-end minor roads, it is worth a visit by those looking for walks off the beaten track. The nearest large town is Hexham, which is always very busy and attracts plenty of visitors, yet very few of them are even aware of the existence of Devil's Water. The valley is flanked on both sides by heather moorlands managed for grouse shooting.

Walking in this area is something best attempted by good navigators. Careful map-reading is required just to find a way through the network of minor roads. More care is needed on the actual walks, since there are few visitors and there is often little sign of a trodden path. Two walks are offered, and they are completely different in character. One of the walks starts near the head of Devil's Water, taking in fiddly field paths and broad heather moorlands around Lilswood Moor and Hangman's Hill. The other walk starts from Dipton Mill, just south of Hexham, where there is access to a jungle-like riverside walk beside Dipton Burn.

Although Hexham has an impressive range of services and is close enough to be considered as a 'gateway' to the North Pennines AONB, it is nevertheless rather removed from the area, sitting squarely beside the River Tyne. There are only tiny villages and hamlets in the valley of Devil's Water, but with a diligent search, there are a few isolated bed and breakfasts and pubs providing at least a few options for accommodation, food and drink. There is no public transport into the valley.

WALK 38

Devil's Water and Hangman Hill

Distance	10.5km (6½ miles)
Terrain	Fiddly field paths give way to a fine moorland track. A vague moorland path is followed by a rugged link back to the start.
Start/finish	Broadwell House – 911536
Maps	OS Landranger 87; Explorer OL43
Refreshments	None.
Transport	None.

Devil's Water and Hangman Hill – it all sounds very sinister, but turns out to be fairly gentle and charming countryside. The route described here passes the end of the road at the head of Devil's Water and makes a circuit around the heathery hump of Lilswood Moor. Perhaps the hardest part of the day involves navigating a network of minor roads to find the starting point.

Was there ever a gibbet erected at Hangman Hill? The location is certainly at a handy point, reached by a number of moorland tracks, yet far enough from habitations for people not to be troubled by living close to a place with such grisly associations.

Broadwell House stands beside the Lilswood Caravan Park on a minor road that runs the length of Devil's Water to Harwood Shield. There is a small parking space beside a telephone kiosk, and the walk starts by following the road uphill.

Watch for a public footpath signpost on the left, revealing a field path leading to **Lilswood Farm**. Keep to the right of the farm to pick up another field path to **Hesleywell**, where there is a farm off a road bend.

Pass the farm buildings to pick up a short path to nearby **New House**, and keep just to the left of it. A couple of ladder-stiles are crossed and the idea is to aim to the right of the farm buildings at **Long Lee** to reach its access road.

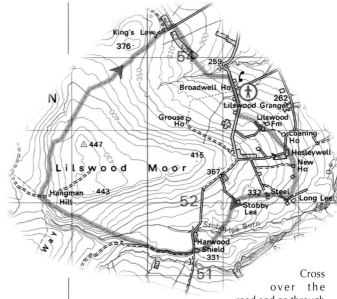

Cross over the road and go through a gate, then climb diag- onally through a rugged field and pass through little gates in front of the house at **Steel**. Watch for a gate on the way through fields beyond, and keep to the right of the farmhouse at **Stobby Lea**. Walk down through fields to cross a footbridge, then climb to reach **Harwood Shield**, going straight through the farm-yard and passing substantial stone outbuildings.

Turn left along the farm access road, then right along a clear track that passes some walled and fenced enclosures on the moorland. The broad moorlands of Hexhamshire Common are designated access land and used for grouse shooting.

After passing the last enclosure, turn right and follow a track down through a gate and across **Stobbylee Burn**. Climb steeply up a stony track to reach a junction on **Hangman Hill**. Turn left downhill and watch for a marker post showing where a bridleway crosses.

Turn right to follow a path gently uphill through the heather. There are often several parallel grooves, so feel free to switch from one to another for the easiest footing. The idea is to follow this series of grooves up and across the broad shoulder of **Lilswood Moor**, almost at 430m (1410ft).

Walk down the other side as if heading down through the valley of Devil's Water. When a wall is reached, keep left of it to reach a corner on a minor road at **King's Law**. Walk down the road a little to cross a cattle-grid beside a stand of forest.

Turn right at a public footpath signpost and cross a ladder-stile at a sheepfold. Walk straight across pathless, rushy ground, beside a strip of moorland planted with tree saplings, to go through a gate. Head down into a bracken-filled valley, cross a stream and climb the other side.

Turn left to walk through heather, reaching a ladder-stile giving access to a minor road. Turn right to pass the caravan park to finish back at **Broadwell House**.

A stone sheepfold is passed before a vague footpath leads back to Broadwell House

WALK 39

Dipton Mill and Dipton Burn

Distance	10km (6 miles)
Terrain	Rugged and well-wooded riverside walking, involving several fords, along with vague, overgrown or muddy paths.
Start/finish	Dipton Mill Inn, near Hexham – 929610
Maps	OS Landranger 87; Explorer OL43
Refreshments	Dipton Mill Inn.
Transport	None to Dipton Mill, though the route can be restructured to start from Nubbock Lodge on the B6305, served by Tynedale buses from Hexham and Allendale Town.

This looks like a fairly straightforward route on a map, but it is actually a jungle trek! The Dipton Mill Inn is a quiet roadside pub south of Hexham, close to Dipton Burn. Paths beside the river near the inn can be rather muddy, but further upstream they dwindle away almost to nothing. Not only that, but to make progress upstream involves fording the river a dozen times or more, so this is definitely not a walk to attempt after heavy rain. The return path stays high above the river and is easier to follow back to the start.

Starting at **Dipton Mill**, take the minor road behind the Dipton Mill Inn and follow it uphill, passing buildings at **Shield Green**, then passing a farm. When the road suddenly turns left, turn right instead to follow a grassy track. This later drops steep and rugged to a footbridge spanning **Dipton Burn**.

Cross over the footbridge and turn left to follow the river upstream, noting how well wooded this narrow valley is. When a path junction is reached, be sure to keep following the river, and not the path running uphill.

There is a vague, trodden path, but it is often overgrown, leading to a crude stepping-stone ford. Not long afterwards, the river has to be forded. Continuing

upstream, the path is narrow and precariously perched above the flow, then becomes easier, before another ford exploits mossy rock in the river.

Progress upstream involves fording **Dipton Burn** over a dozen times, and it is quite likely that this will result in wet feet. However, for those who enjoy forging through jungle-like surroundings, this is rather a special route.

Eventually, it becomes necessary to climb up a short, steep slope to reach the northern brow of the river valley. Anyone missing this climb will quickly reach a minor road spanning the river below

The Dipton Mill Inn is submerged in greenery at the start of the walk

191

Nubbock Lodge, in which case turn right up it, then right again as signposted along a footpath.

The path stays close to a drystone wall at the edge of the wood, so that there are occasional glimpses of fields beyond. Sometimes the path is rather narrow and can be overgrown with bracken, but it is in much better shape than the riverside path below. The tallest trees are mighty beeches, but the woods are quite mixed throughout.

When a bridleway marker is spotted, the route is not far from **Hexham Racecourse**, though this cannot be seen without making a detour. Keep right and head gently uphill, then walk down through a groove cut into soft sandstone, which carries water when wet. The path leads down to **Dipton Burn** and reaches the footbridge that was crossed earlier in the day.

Do not cross the river, but follow a path downstream. This muddy way leads to a couple of fords, but these can be avoided, provided that left turns are made in advance of each ford. One stretch runs out of the woods, through a flowery meadow, then back into the woods.

Walking beside Dipton Burn is like following a jungle trek through dense woodlands

The last part of the path can be very muddy when wet, passing a small waterfall before reaching a road bridge. Turn right and cross the bridge to finish back at the Dipton Mill Inn.

Section 11
ALLENDALE

There are actually two Allendales. The East Allen stretches from Allenhead to Allendale Town and the Cupola Bridge. The West Allen includes the tiny settlements of Ninebanks and Whitfield, also stretching to the Cupola Bridge. The River East Allen and River West Allen become simply the River Allen as they flow through a deep and delightfully well-wooded gorge to reach the River Tyne. The gorge at Allen Banks is the most northerly part of the North Pennines AONB, and the only area of any extent owned by the National Trust.

Four remarkably different walks explore this area. The first takes advantage of paths that seldom appear on any maps, exploring the deepest recesses of Allen Banks and the Staward Gorge. This is an intensely interesting place, full of fiddly paths and curiosities, as well as being a haven for wildlife. Allendale Town is well placed for exploring high moorlands. A circular – or more correctly, triangular – walk wanders over the broad heather moors of Hexhamshire Common, which is a notable grouse-shooting area. The moorland trek gives way to a charming riverside walk. On the other side of Allendale Town, old stone-built flues stretch from the site of a smelt mill deep in the dale, up to the moors high above, where noxious fumes could be safely vented. Over in West Allendale, a short or long circuit can be walked from Ninebanks, stretching from the pastoral valley to the broad and boggy moors high above.

Allendale Town is a natural base for exploring this area of the North Pennines, featuring a limited but adequate range of facilities, as well as a bus service linking with Hexham. However, if relying on public transport, it is necessary to link together several schedules to gain access to all the walks in this area.

WALK 40
Allen Banks and Staward Gorge

Distance	14km (8¾ miles)
Terrain	Winding riverside paths and narrow paths on steep, wooded slopes.
Start/finish	Allen Banks car park – 798640
Maps	OS Landranger 86 or 87; OS Explorer OL43
Refreshments	Pub off-route from Staward.
Public Transport	Nearby Bardon Mill has regular trains as well as Arriva and Stagecoach buses from Carlisle and Newcastle. Wright Brothers buses pass Staward in summer, linking with Hexham and Alston.

Allen Banks and Staward Gorge feature ancient woodland, and this is the only National Trust property of any size in the North Pennines. Susan Davidson, who was related to the Bowes-Lyon family, lived at Ridley Hall in the mid-19th century. She oversaw the creation of 'wilderness walks' at Allen Banks. Trees were cut down and paths were laid, along with stone steps and strategically sited summerhouses. Wild flowers and wildlife abound, including lush growths of garlic-scented ramsons in spring and the chance to spot deer. The estate was donated to the National Trust by Francis Bowes-Lyon in 1942.

Start at the National Trust car park at **Allen Banks**, which is located in a former walled garden attached to nearby Ridley Hall. Follow a splendidly easy path upstream beside the **River Allen**, marvelling at the wooded gorge on the way to a suspension footbridge. Cross the bridge and climb straight up a flight of stone steps on a steep and wooded slope.

Turn right as marked by the word 'tarn' on a stone, and the path winds uphill to join a clearer path. Cross over this and climb up more stone steps, then, when the path drops a little to a junction, turn right uphill as marked 'tarn' again. Higher uphill, a post with the word 'tarn' indicates a left turn. The path climbs from oaks to pines, with masses of rhododendron, then a short walk leads down to **Morralee Tarn**.

Walk to the outflow of this little pool and turn left onto a lesser path, which later swings left to traverse a wooded slope and returns to the post marked with the word 'tarn'. Retrace steps back down to the suspension footbridge, but do not cross. Instead, turn left to follow a rugged path upstream beside the **River Allen**.

The path runs up and down steps, passing mossy boulders, eventually crossing a stile to pass a riverside meadow. When the path joins a track, turn right to follow it uphill a little to join a road. Turn right to follow the road down to **Plankey Mill**, where a meadow provides a basic campsite.

It is possible to cross a footbridge and return directly to Allen Banks, but to explore further, keep walking upstream through the meadow. Enter woodland again and follow a rugged riverside path, later crossing a footbridge over a stream. Looking across the river, cliffs rise from the water. A path junction is reached, so keep right to follow the river into steep-sided **Staward Gorge**. (The route returns down the other path later.)

STAWARD GORGE

This National Trust property contains ancient woodlands, but non-native beeches and conifers are also present. There is a long-term plan to fell most nonnative trees and replant native species. The ground cover in the ancient parts includes moscatel, wood fescue, woodruff and hard shield fern. Woodland

195

birds include tawny owls, wood warblers and willow tits. The river supports dippers, grey wagtails, goosanders and oystercatchers. The most northerly colony of dormice lives in the gorge, while with patience an otter might be spotted.

The path is rough and narrow in places, clinging to a steep, wooded slope overlooking the river. Take care, as a crag along the way occasionally drops rocks onto the path. Keep walking, and the path eventually climbs high above the flow, reaching a junction at a stile on the top of the wooded slope above the **Cupola Bridge**.

Cross the stile into a rough-pasture field and turn left. Follow the edge of the field to a stile and step onto the **A686** again. Turn left to follow the road past an enormous stone wall to reach Staward Station (weekend bed and breakfast available) on the old Hexham to Allendale railway. ◄

The Carts Bog Inn is further along the main road if food or drink is required.

Go through a gate on the left, as signposted, and walk down through rough pasture. Go through another gate and climb gently to a ruin called **Gingle Pot**, formerly a cattle drovers' inn. Go through a gateway and follow a drystone wall roughly northwards. A grassy path runs alongside, while the rest of the field is rushy.

The path runs towards a forest then splits into two. Take the path on the left, gently downhill to a gate where there is a National Trust sign for Staward Gorge. The path runs along a narrow, steep-sided, well-wooded ridge between Allendale and Harsondale, reaching the ruins of **Staward Peel**.

STAWARD PEEL

From 1272 until 1384, Staward Peel was a stronghold, and well nigh impregnable in such a location. From 1384 it was used by hermits from the Priory of Hexham as a place for retreat and prayer. It remained a property of the Church until the Dissolution of 1539. In 1613, King James I granted the ruins to Lord Howard de Walden, who stripped the stonework to build nearby Staward Manor.

Follow a path steeply downhill into denser woods, turning right at a junction to reach the **River Allen** at a point passed earlier in the walk. Retrace steps by crossing a footbridge over a stream and continue down through the valley. The path can be rugged as it traverses steep, wooded slopes. The path becomes easier, leaves the forest and runs through a meadow to return to **Plankey Mill**.

A suspension footbridge once spanned the River Allen here, but it was dismantled and a new girder-and-wood bridge built nearby. Cross over it and turn right to cross a smaller footbridge over a stream. Enter the little **Briarwood Banks** nature reserve, which is an ancient oak and ash wood, with some hazel coppice. A National Trust sign is passed as the path continues downstream.

The riverside path is quite easy, then it passes a sheer cliff of sandstone and enters a more restrictive part of the gorge. Pass the suspension footbridge used earlier in the day, and keep straight ahead to return to the car park at **Allen Banks.**

Towards the end of the walk, a fine path runs back to Allen Banks, beside the River Allen

WALK 41
Allendale Town and Hexhamshire Common

Distance	16km (10 miles)
Terrain	Good tracks and occasional vague paths across broad heather moorlands, followed by riverside paths and field paths.
Start/finish	Allendale Town – 837558
Maps	OS Landranger 87; Explorer OL43
Refreshments	Plenty of choice at Allendale Town.
Transport	Tynedale buses run daily, except Sundays, from Hexham to Allendale Town.

Hexhamshire Common is a broad and gently undulating expanse of heather moorland between Allendale and Devil's Water. It is primarily grouse-shooting country, but is also designated access land and comprehensively crisscrossed by public bridleways. The area is a joy to explore in summer when the heather is flushed purple, but it can be just as good on a good winter's day.

Starting from Allendale Town, two bridleways are used to cross the moor, then pleasant paths are followed downstream beside the River East Allen.

Leave **Allendale Town** by following the road signposted for Hexham, but quickly turn right up Shilburn Road. Follow the road uphill, passing **High Struthers** to reach the end of the tarmac, where a gate gives way to open moorland.

A signpost at this point reads 'Hexhamshire' and a stony track leads onto the moors, rising gently beside a wall at first. Later, the track bends left for **Crawberry Hill**, so leave it to follow a grassy track straight ahead over the heather moors. There are ruts and boggy patches as the track leads gently down towards a green hut beside a gate on **Burntridge Moor**.

Turn right at a signpost before reaching the hut, as indicated for East Allen Dale. A grassy track rises gently, running parallel to a wall on heather moorland over-looking a farm at **Westburnhope**. Drop a little to cross a stream, then the track becomes stony and rutted as it drifts away from the wall and climbs to a lonely signpost at **Stobb Cross**.

Allendale Town is signposted to the right, and this could serve as a short-cut, but keep straight ahead as signposted for Sinderhope to continue the walk. The path is quite rutted as it rises gently through heather, and if unsure of its course, keep well to the left of **Green Hill** and its conspicuous plantation. The path climbs as high as 410m (1345ft) and follows a drystone wall down to a gate.

Leave the moorland and follow a minor road down to the B6295 at **Sinderhope**. Turn right and follow the road up past a converted chapel, then watch for a sign-post on the left revealing a vague path down a steep and well-wooded slope. Head upstream beside the **River East Allen** and cross a footbridge with a fine view of a waterfall.

A gentle stretch of the River East Allen between Park and Allendale Town

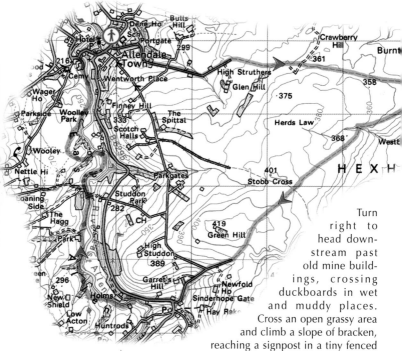

Turn right to head downstream past old mine buildings, crossing duckboards in wet and muddy places. Cross an open grassy area and climb a slope of bracken, reaching a signpost in a tiny fenced enclosure. Turn right downhill as indicated for Park. The path crosses footbridges over a couple of streams in little valleys, then keeps right of the farm buildings at **Park**.

Continue as marked, walking roughly parallel to the **River East Allen**, though it is seldom seen because of trees and bushes alongside. Pass an unsafe bridge, then at the next footbridge, it is possible to cross the river and follow a path and road straight back to Allendale Town.

To stay on the main route, however, don't cross the footbridge, but head downstream and cross a footbridge over an inflowing stream instead. Turn left to climb uphill, keeping left of a house and passing through a gate.

Watch out for markers that generally indicate a series of right turns, taking the route through fields and back towards the river.

The path actually stays high above the **River East Allen**, gradually descending towards some buildings, then following an access road downstream. Turn right to cross a stone-arch bridge over the river and climb straight back into the middle of **Allendale Town.** This is the main population centre in the area, and has a small but adequate range of facilities.

ALLENDALE TOWN TAR BARLING

New Year's Eve is referred to as Old Year's Night in Allendale, and the local folk celebrate it with a stirring fire festival. Tough-looking dalesfolk don fancy dress and are known as 'guisers'. They carry blazing tar barrels on their heads and process round town, hurling the barrels onto a central bonfire as the church bells ring in the New Year. After frantically 'first footing' round all the houses, the local folk melt away, leaving hordes of visiting tourists wondering what happened! Be warned that not a bed is to be had in the area during 'tar barling'.

WALK 42
Allendale Town and Allenmill Flues

Distance	12km (7½ miles)
Terrain	Roads, tracks and paths lead to high moorlands, with roads leading back.
Start/finish	Allendale Town – 837558
Maps	OS Landranger 86 or 87; Explorer OL43
Refreshments	Plenty of choice at Allendale Town.
Transport	Tynedale buses run daily, except Sundays, from Hexham to Allendale Town.

Allendale Town, formerly known as Allenton, was granted a charter by Edward I. Lead mining was an important industry, but the ore contained a significant amount of silver too. In the mid-19th century Allendale's population expanded and a smelt mill was constructed at Allenmill. In earlier times, smelt mills discharged poisonous fumes into populated areas, but in 1778 Bishop Watson pressed for the construction of long flues to carry fumes far from the mills to be vented elsewhere. The remains of old flues can be found all around the North Pennines, but the ones above Allendale are particularly well preserved.

Follow a road downhill to leave **Allendale Town** passing the Hare and Hounds pub. A path short-cuts a road bend, but watch for another path on the right, signposted for Oakpool. The walk downstream beside the **River East Allen** is quite popular.

Pass an old mine building and note the stream flowing from a level with a grille across it. Further along the wooded path a stone abutment once supported a railway bridge linking Allendale with Hexham.

Turn left to follow the **B6295** across a twin-arched bridge, passing the site of the Allenmill smelt mill, following the road up to **Thornley Gate** and a complex road junction. Take the road signposted for Ninebanks.

An intact stretch of the Allenmill Flue, beside the Carrier's Way above Fell House

The road passes a farm at a point where the old flue once crossed, though there is no trace of it today. Continue further up the road to another house and turn left up a track signposted as a public byway, alongside **Oakeydean Burn**.

Halfway to the next road, look out on the right for two old flues diverging and heading for the high moors. Turn right along the road, passing a farm to reach a road junction. Turn left up a road between the lines of the two old flues. While climbing the road, the flue of the left moves further away, while the flue on the right draws closer. Cross a cattle-grid to reach a final habitation, white **Fell House**.

A grass-covered flue rises onto the moors, with a track called the Carriers Way alongside. ▶ There are two **chimneys** on the high moors – a tall and slender one off to the left – with a short and broad-based one ahead.

Some parts of the flue have collapsed, while the stonework in other parts survives intact. Beware of getting too close, as the structure is unsafe.

ALLENMILL FLUES

Noxious fumes generated at Allenmill were conducted up through stone-built flues to be vented through chimneys on the moors. Lead smelting was essentially a matter of heating galena to drive off sulphur and leave the lead behind. However, the process needed careful control. It was a waste of fuel if too little or too much heat was generated, or if too little or too much air

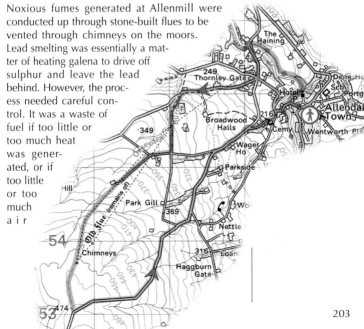

was introduced. The construction of a flue, while expensive, was good for the health of local people, and also allowed valuable substances to condense on its stone walls. From time to time the flues would be cleaned out by young lads and the substances gathered were sent for further refinement.

Continue beyond the short and broad-based chimney to follow a squelchy, grassy path across **Dryburn Moor** and up to a minor road. Turn left to follow the road down into Allendale, always keeping straight ahead at three road junctions, but remembering to turn right at a fourth.

There is no signpost, but this steep and narrow road offers a good short-cut down to the **River East Allen**. Cross a stone-arch bridge over the river and climb straight back into the middle of **Allendale Town**.

WALK 43
Ninebanks, Hard Rigg and the Dodd

Distance	11 or 20km (7 or 12½ miles)
Terrain	A good track at the start, then broad and boggy moorland with walls and fences as guides. Open moorland with vague paths before the end.
Start/finish	Ninebanks Youth Hostel – 771514
Maps	OS Landranger 87; Explorers OL31 and OL43
Refreshments	None.
Transport	Occasional Wright Brothers buses link Ninebanks with Newcastle, Alston, Penrith and Keswick in the summer.

Several rights of way climb onto the moors above Ninebanks. Some are clear tracks, while others are vague paths, or even completely untrodden. No rights of way run along the high moorland crest at the head of West Allen Dale, but all the high ground is access land, while drystone walls and post-and wire fences offer faultless guides, marking the county boundary between Northumberland and Cumbria.

A fairly easy circuit can be enjoyed over Hard Rigg, or a longer and harder route can be followed over the Dodd.

Ninebanks Youth Hostel, housed in a 17th-century lead-miner's cottage, is an ideal base for this walk. Leave the hostel to walk down the road and round a bend. Turn left up a clear track signposted as a public byway.

The track climbs rough and stony, enclosed by grassy banks and drystone walls, while looking back downhill reveals a glimpse of the church spire at Ninebanks. Looking ahead, the track levels out at a sheepfold where a gate leads onto a moor. Climb gently along the track, then drop down a little to cross a bridge over **Sandyford Sike**. Climb gently to reach a gate and a forest at **Long Cross**.

Don't go through the gate, but turn left to follow the forest fence. A firm limestone footing gives way to a level,

Gentle riverside walking can be enjoyed on the way back to Ninebanks

205

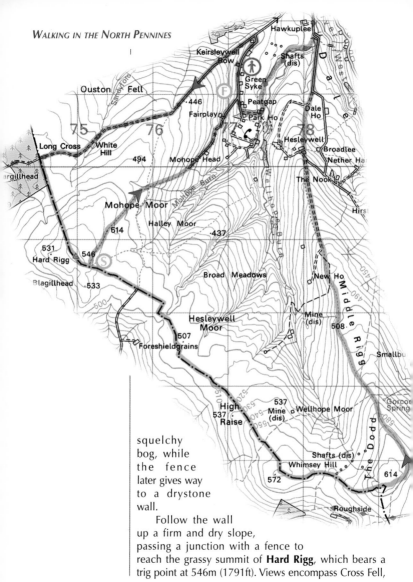

squelchy bog, while the fence later gives way to a drystone wall.

Follow the wall up a firm and dry slope, passing a junction with a fence to reach the grassy summit of **Hard Rigg**, which bears a trig point at 546m (1791ft). Views encompass Cross Fell,

Alston Moor, Cold Fell, Whitfield Moor, Allendale and the Dodd.

Follow the wall gently downhill, where a fence continues across a broad dip. Another stretch of wall crosses a gentle rise, then there is another short stretch of fence. A wall crosses a little hump and lands beside a gate at **Blacklaw Cross**. At this point the walk can be finished early, or it can be extended considerably.

To finish early, turn left, away from the gate, to follow a vague path, known as the Carriers Way, across the moors. The path is identified by a line of marker posts, and while these can be seen ahead in clear weather, they need to be watched for with care in mist. Spot each one in turn, then look for the next one in line, as the 'path' is nothing more than a vague, boggy groove on **Mohope Moor**.

Gradually the path swings right and drops down to the nearest trees in view. It becomes enclosed and is easier to follow down to **Fairplay**. Continue down the farm road and turn left at the bottom to return to **Ninebanks Youth Hostel**.

To stay on the main route, simply keep to the left-hand side of the drystone wall, heading for **Hesleywell Moor**. The wall suddenly turns a corner and the ground is appallingly boggy, so pick any course with a view to keeping your feet dry.

Later, the wall leads off the main moorland crest, so follow a fence instead, which also turns a corner, then continue along the line of the wall afterwards. It runs more directly along the moorland crest, passing a gateway where a fence joins, then climbing onto firmer ground on **High Raise**.

There is a gate in the wall, where a fine, firm, grassy track crosses, leading left over to a lead mine and shooting huts, and right towards Nentshead.

Keep following the wall to cross **Whimsey Hill**, at 572m (1877ft), passing an old lead-mine spoil on the other side. The wall has been rebuilt across a broad dip, and it crosses a right of way and a rusty pipeline. Follow the wall uphill again, almost to the summit of **The Dodd** at 614m (2014ft). Enjoy extensive views, and also note the sudden appearance of the village of Nentshead below.

Follow the wall off the summit, but when it starts dropping steeply, watch out for a path rising gently to the left, bearing a couple of marker posts. Follow this path and it becomes broad and grassy, high on the Dodd, no longer requiring marker posts. However, there are a couple of moves ahead that require care, especially in mist.

First, the track forks, so keep right as marked, but watch out for a tall, columnar cairn away to the left later, and walk towards it. Look ahead along the broad and grassy moorland crest of **Middle Rigg** to spot a grassy groove of a path. Follow this line to reach the corner of a wall.

From the corner, either walk straight ahead using the wall as a guide, or keep following the grassy groove at a higher level. Both lines cross wet and rushy patches, and both meet where a grassy access track rises from the isolated farm of **New House**.

Follow the track straight ahead, later going through a gate and continuing to a road end. A house is hidden in trees ahead. Approach it, but turn left as signposted to find a track and field path leading to a farm at **Hesleywell**.

Turn right on reaching the farm, but just before leaving it, turn left and right to locate a path leading down into a wooded valley. Cross the confluence of Wellhope Burn and **Mohope Burn** and climb up to a road. Turn right to follow the road, which itself turns left and right later to return to **Ninebanks Youth Hostel**.

Section 12
SOUTH TYNEDALE

The River South Tyne is well known among those who walk the Pennine Way, since they follow it from Garrigill to Alston, onwards past Slaggyford, and out of the North Pennines altogether. Alston has the reputation of being the highest market town in England, and is the largest town completely inside the North Pennines AONB. Stanhope and Middleton-in-Teesdale, its nearest rivals, lie slightly outside the boundary of the AONB. Some of the highest roads in England converge on Alston, so in the winter months approaches can be blocked by snow, leaving only the valley route open through South Tynedale.

Three walks are described in this area, each remarkably different from the others. An easy series of farm tracks and field paths can be linked on a walk from Alston to Garrigill and back again. The return journey uses the Pennine Way, and the South Tyne Trail

piggybacks onto the same route. A long but easy walk follows an old railway trackbed running the length of South Tynedale, from Alston, past Slaggyford and Lambley, leaving the North Pennines AONB to reach Haltwhistle. The third route starts easily, following a fine track away from Slaggyford, but it traverses broad and bleak moorlands in search of Tom Smith's Stone, before crossing Grey Nag and finding its way back down into South Tynedale.

Alston is the natural base for exploring South Tynedale, boasting a splendid range of services and facilities. Its main shopping street is alarmingly steep but full of character. Bus services are enhanced in the summer months, when Alston can be reached directly from points as far removed as Newcastle and Keswick, on a daily basis. Nearby villages have rather limited facilities, but most can provide accommodation, food and drink.

WALK 44

Alston, Garrigill and River South Tyne

Distance	14km (8¾ miles)
Terrain	Low-level farm tracks, field paths and occasional roads.
Start/finish	Market cross, Alston – 718465
Maps	OS Landranger 86; Explorer OL31
Refreshments	Plenty of choice at Alston. Pub at Garrigill.
Transport	Daily Stagecoach buses link Alston with Carlisle, except Sundays. Daily Tynedale buses link Alston with Haltwhistle, except Sundays. Wright Brothers buses link Alston and Garrigill on schooldays, and also operate a summer service linking Alston with Keswick, Penrith, Hexham and Newcastle.

This is a fairly simple circuit between Alston and Garrigill, running close to the River South Tyne. The outward journey is along farm tracks and vague field paths, while the return journey is along the Pennine Way, which also doubles as the South Tyne Trail. The walk leaves the top end of Alston and returns at the bottom end, so there is an opportunity to explore the whole of the town before or after the walk.

Start in the middle of **Alston**, at Market Cross on steep, cobbled Front Street. Follow the road uphill, but watch for the Swans Head and old Wesleyan chapel on the right, and walk between them. A tarmac path is flanked by drystone walls and is signposted for Nattrass Gill. Follow it more or less level to its end, then turn left and quickly right to continue along a farm access road, also signposted for Nattrass Gill.

The road passes **Fairhill** and reaches old buildings at **Annat Walls**, where past inhabitants were 'careful to arrange axes and other weapons at the heads of their beds in order to be in readiness to defend their property against the Scots'.

Continue alongside a wall through a field, then drop down stone steps into the wooded ravine of **Nattrass Gill**, looking out for wood sorrel, ramsons and dainty ferns. Cross two footbridges and catch a glimpse of waterfalls before climbing stone steps to emerge in fields again.

Tall marker posts show the location of stiles as the path leads onwards, well to the left of a house at **Nest**. Turn left along the access road, then right at a junction, heading down another access road to **Bleagate**. There is a glimpse of distant Cross Fell on the descent.

Turn left along the Pennine Way, following a field path over a rise to reach a farmhouse at **Sillyhall**. The Pennine Way heads right at a fork, so keep left instead to go through a small gate. (The Pennine Way will be used again here on the return.)

Walk straight ahead alongside fields, keeping an eye open for little stone stiles and marker arrows. Pass a small stone ruin beside an old lead mine, then keep to the left of farm buildings at **Low Crag**.

Watch for tall marker posts on the way through more fields, passing well below another farm, and later crossing

One of the old buildings passed at Annat Walls on the way from Alston to Garrigill

211

a footbridge over a narrow, wooded ravine. Follow a wall to its end, then drift left uphill to reach a road beside a **cemetery**.

Turn right along the road and follow it down past an old Wesleyan chapel, where there is a tea room, blacksmith's forge and a waterfall. The road continues down to the village of **Garrigill**.

GARRIGILL

Garrigill is a quiet village beside the River South Tyne, arranged round a large green boasting some fine trees. Facilities include the George and Dragon Inn, a post office shop and a handful of bed and breakfasts. Camping is available on a tiny plot behind the village hall in exchange for a small donation. There is, rather surprisingly, a small swimming pool and sauna available at St John's Hall beside the church.

Leave **Garrigill** along the road signposted for Leadgate to return to Alston along the Pennine Way. The road runs beside the **River South Tyne**, but when it climbs above it, follow a riverside path instead, passing an area of mining spoil. The path climbs above the river for a while, then descends and runs closer to it, reaching a **footbridge**.

Cross over the **River South Tyne** and turn left, following the path away from the river to reach the farmhouse at **Sillyhall** again. Follow a field path over a rise to return to **Bleagate**, then turn left between the buildings and right to continue through fields.

The path stays away from the river and crosses several stone stiles. These stiles have been rebuilt and reinforced to cope with the number of people following the Pennine Way. The foot of **Nattrass Gill** is hardly noticed on this part of the route.

The last stretch of path is a wooded walk above the river, known as the Firs, reaching a youth hostel. Either follow the main road back into the lower part of **Alston**, or climb a flight of steps just before that point to follow a tarmac path to the old Wesleyan chapel at the top of the town.

ALSTON

Alston claims to be the highest market town in England, rising from the banks of the River South Tyne at 280m (920ft) to 320m (1050ft) at the primary school at the top of the town. Most of Alston's shops and services are arranged beside steep, cobbled Front Street, where a shopping trip needs careful planning to avoid unnecessary ascents and descents! Alston has one of the best ranges of services and facilities in the North Pennines, with a tourist information centre in the town hall, tel 01434 382244.

Market Cross in the centre of town is essentially a roof supported on stone pillars. It has been demolished by runaway trucks not once, but twice. It was gifted to the town in 1765 by William Stephenson, an Alston man who became Lord Mayor of London. St Augustine's Church is easily spotted because of its tall tower. Several fine stone buildings have been erected by public subscription. It is well worth wandering round quaint and poky back alleys, such as the Butts, once used for archery practice, and Gossipgate.

WALK 45

Alston, Lambley and Haltwhistle

Distance	23km (14¼ miles)
Terrain	Easy, level, firm trackbed through cultivated countryside and woods.
Start	South Tyne Railway, Alston – 717467
Finish	Haltwhistle – 705641
Maps	OS Landranger 86 or 87; Explorer OL31 and OL43
Refreshments	Plenty of choice at Alston. Buffet carriage available at Kirkhaugh Station when the train arrives. Pubs off-route at Knarsdale and Featherstone Park. Plenty of choice at Haltwhistle.
Transport	The South Tyne Railway links Alston and Kirkhaugh. Daily Stagecoach buses run from Alston to Slaggyford, except Sundays, passing close to Lambley on the way to Carlisle. Daily Tynedale buses run between Haltwhistle, Coanwood and Alston, except Sundays. Regular daily Arriva and Stagecoach buses, as well as trains, link Haltwhistle with Carlisle and Newcastle.

For many years the Pennine Way led walkers through gentle South Tynedale, but more recently an old railway trackbed has been cleared for the use of walkers and cyclists, as part of the South Tyne Trail, leading all the way from Alston to Haltwhistle. The narrow-gauge South Tyne Railway operates along the first part of the line, while old station sites and abandoned platforms are passed later. This splendidly easy linear walk would appeal to 'railway ramblers', because of its railway heritage from start to finish.

SOUTH TYNE RAILWAY

The Newcastle & Carlisle Railway Company originally planned to construct a railway from Haltwhistle to the lead mines at Nenthead, but later decided to terminate the line at Alston, abandoning what would have been a steep climb onwards. The line was

constructed between 1851 and 1852, featuring nine viaducts spanning the River South Tyne and some of its tributaries. Apart from transporting lead ore, the railway also carried passengers until closure in 1976.

The South Tyne Railway Preservation Society, tel 01434 381696, www.strps.co.uk, now operates a narrow-gauge railway along the old trackbed from Alston. At the time of writing, their line terminates at Kirkhaugh, but an extension is planned to reach Slaggyford. Beyond Slaggyford the trackbed has been resurfaced and is popular with cyclists as well as walkers.

The South Tyne Trail runs parallel to the South Tyne Railway between Alston and Kirkhaugh.

Start at the lower end of **Alston,** where the South Tyne Railway station is located, along with the Hub museum and a café. Use a level crossing, then turn right to walk parallel to the railway, following a gravel path past a picnic site and across a buttress above the **River South Tyne**.

Later, cross the line and use a path running parallel on the other side. Cross a viaduct over the river and follow the line as it curves and runs under a stone-arch bridge.

After passing another stone-arch bridge, the line crosses a viaduct over **Gilderdale Burn**. Go through a short, wooded cutting, which is directly below Whitley Castle, a Roman fort on the shoulder of a hill. Cross a short viaduct over a wooded valley to reach **Kirkhaugh Station**. There is only a platform here, but when trains arrive they haul a buffet carriage dispensing snacks.

Walk under a stone-arch bridge to pass the end of the railway line (but bear in mind that there is a plan to extend it onwards). Cross a bridge over a track at **Kirkhaugh**, then follow the trackbed round a bend and pass under a bridge. Throughout this stretch, the Pennine Way runs roughly parallel through fields.

An embankment, a cutting and another embankment are passed on the way to **Lintley**, where a farm sits on a knoll. Cross a viaduct here, then pass under a skew arch carrying the **A689**. A soft cutting leads onto an embankment with three bridges beneath it, then the trackbed goes through another cutting, under a bridge, over a bridge, finally reaching a road at **Slaggyford**. There is a bed and breakfast down the road, as well as access to bus services on the main road.

Pass the old railway station to leave the village, and the

trackbed gains a tarmac surface, passing under a bridge in wooded surroundings. Cross a short viaduct to emerge from the woods, then go through a wooded cutting and pass under a strengthened road bridge.

map continued
on page 219

Later, cross a bridge over a river and a road at **Knarsdale**, where the Kirkstyle Inn can be reached off-route, offering food, drink and accommodation.

A wooded stretch of the trackbed runs parallel to the **A689**, through a cutting and across a bridge to pass a farm at **Softley**. Cross a wooded valley, continue through woodland, then cross another wooded valley to emerge among fields at **Whitwham**. A notice beside a gate tells walkers to keep a lookout for lapwing, curlew, snipe, oystercatcher and redshank in the fields. Another wooded stretch leads towards the old station near **Lambley**.

There is no access to the station, so head down steps to the right beforehand, almost to the River South Tyne, then climb up steps to pass under one of the towering arches of **Lambley Viaduct**, keeping left up more steps to regain the old trackbed on top. Cross the viaduct and admire fine views of the river and its wooded surroundings at this point.

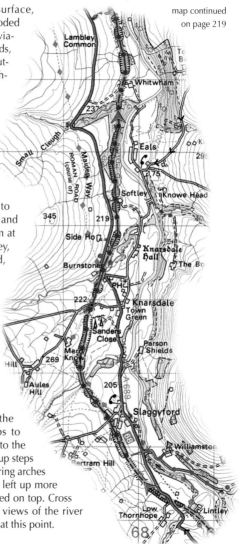

Walking high above the River South Tyne while following the South Tyne Trail across the Lambley Viaduct

LAMBLEY VIADUCT

This viaduct is monumental, and the most striking feature of the South Tyne Trail. It was opened on 17 November 1852, having been built using sandstone from Slaggyford and Bardon Mill. It rises 32m (105ft) above the River South Tyne, spanning it with nine main arches and seven smaller ones. The largest block of stone used in its construction weighed 950kg (1 ton). A pedestrian footbridge was once attached to the stonework, but later dismantled. Following the viaduct's restoration in 1995, visitors now walk more comfortably between the flanking walls.

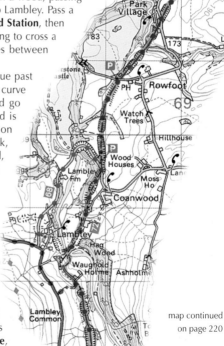

The trackbed runs through a wood, passing a cottage with a view back to Lambley. Pass a platform at the old **Coanwood Station**, then head through a wooded cutting to cross a road used by Tynedale buses between Haltwhistle and Alston.

Pass a car park to continue past the site of a coke works, then curve round through a cutting and go under a bridge. When a road is reached beside the old station house at Featherstone Park, the Wallace Arms offers food, drink and accommodation just to the right in the direction of **Rowfoot**.

The trackbed leads through a grassy, flowery cutting that was once spanned by a bridge, then follows a wooded embankment over a wooded valley, rather like following an avenue flanked by birch trees.

Go under a road and almost immediately cross another road at **Park Village**,

map continued on page 220

219

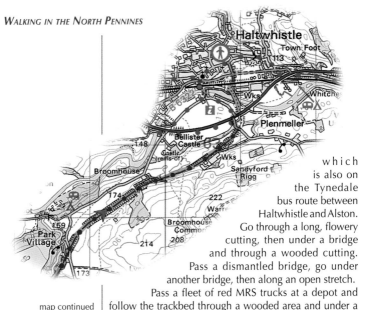

which is also on the Tynedale bus route between Haltwhistle and Alston. Go through a long, flowery cutting, then under a bridge and through a wooded cutting. Pass a dismantled bridge, go under another bridge, then along an open stretch.

map continued from page 219

Pass a fleet of red MRS trucks at a depot and follow the trackbed through a wooded area and under a bridge. The end of the line is reached suddenly at a road. Cross the road and turn left down to the busy **A69**.

Turn right as if for Newcastle, then cross over to pick up a 'wildlife corridor' path onto the Alston Arches Viaduct. This spans the **River South Tyne**, but leads to a barrier. Drop down to the right and pick up a road leading straight into **Haltwhistle**, and turn left to reach the town centre.

HALTWHISTLE

Haltwhistle claims to be the 'centre of Britain' – along with other contenders in widely different parts of the country. It is a busy little town with a full range of facilities and a tourist information centre, tel 01434 322002.

WALK 46

Slaggyford and Grey Nag

Distance	20km (12½ miles)
Terrain	A firm track leads onto boggy moorland where fences make useful guides. A rugged descent beside a river links with field paths and an old railway trackbed.
Start/finish	Slaggyford – 677524
Maps	OS Landranger 86; Explorers OL31 and OL43
Refreshments	Buffet carriage available at Kirkhaugh Station when the train arrives.
Transport	Daily Stagecoach and Wright Brothers buses link Slaggyford with Alston, Brampton and Carlisle, except Sundays.

A fine track runs from Slaggyford into Knarsdale, and this has recently been extended for grouse shooting. The moors are designated access land, and while they seem bleak and remote, route-finding is simply a matter of following fences and walls one after the other. The curious Tom Smith's Stone can be inspected on the way to the broad top of Grey Nag. The descent is rugged in places, linking with the Pennine Way, but a level railway trackbed can be used to return to Slaggyford.

Slaggyford is a small village arranged around a green. Only one road rises above the green, passing the Yew Tree Chapel bed and breakfast and old railway station. Follow the road uphill, but as soon as it drops downhill, turn left up a track marked 'private'.

Keep right of a house on **Bertram Hill** and follow a clear track further uphill. ▶ The track is enclosed by walls or fences as it undulates gently across the eastern flanks of **Knarsdale.**

A shooting cabin is reached where the track once ended at a gate, but two recently constructed tracks continue onwards. Keep left at a junction, later passing above a solitary shepherd's hut at **High Shield**, and below

A notice erected by the Knarsdale Estates asks visitors to keep dogs on leads.

a stone chimney stack where a former shooting hut was demolished. The track ends suddenly, leaving a rather awkward, muddy crossing of two little streams.

A prominent fence continues onwards, up a boggy moorland slope of heather, bilberry and bog cotton. Follow it faithfully to reach a junction with another fence on the main Pennine watershed, which also carries the county boundary between Northumberland and Cumbria.

Don't cross any of the fences, but turn left to follow the county boundary fence a little further uphill. ◀ Another junction of fences is reached at **Tom Smith's Stone**, at 631m (2071ft).

Cloudberries grow abundantly on the permanently wet peat.

TOM SMITH'S STONE

The letters A, C, K and W are carved on the faces of Tom Smith's Stone, corresponding to Alston, Croglin, Knarsdale and Whitley. Only three boundary fences meet here, but the rotting remains of a fourth fence can be distinguished to the southeast. Who was Tom Smith? Was he the man who carried the stone to this point and planted it in the bog? Was he the man who paid for the stone and ordered it to be planted?

Enjoy views from Cold Fell to Cross Fell while pondering why anyone would mark a boundary in such a bleak and remote place.

Turn left to head northeast, following a fence away from Tom Smith's Stone. The moorland crest remains boggy as it rises and falls gently, then it becomes firm and heathery underfoot as a drystone wall climbs uphill.

If you are still walking on the left-hand side of the fence, it is a good idea to cross so that you continue along the right-hand side of the wall. Simply follow the wall to a sheepfold in a corner, close to the summit of **Grey Nag** at 656m (2152ft). The cairn is part of the wall and there is a trig point beside it.

Turn right to follow
the wall a short way
east, then right
again to fol-
low a fence
roughly
south-
east

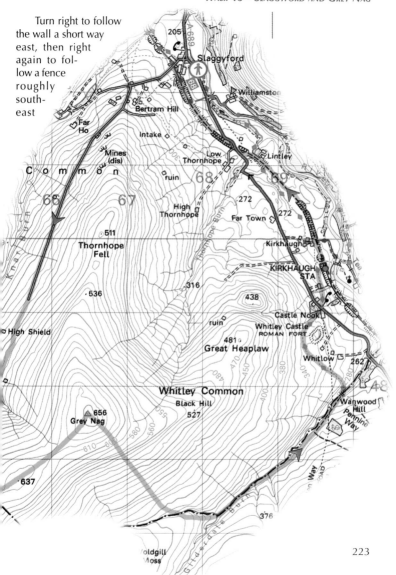

205

A689

Slaggyford

Williamston

Bertram Hill

Far
Ho

Intake

Lintley

Mines
(dis)

Low
Thornhope

C o m m o n

ruin

68

69

68

67

272

High
Thornhope

272

Far Town

511

Knar Burn

Thornhope
Fell

Kirkhaugh

KIRKHAUGH
STA

536

316

438

Tees

High Shield

ruin

Castle Nook

Whitley Castle
ROMAN FORT

481

Great Heaplaw

Whitlow

262

Whitley Common

Black Hill

527

Wanwood
Hill
Pennine
Way

656
Grey Nag

Way

ROAD

637

oldgill
Moss

Gilderdale Burn

376

223

downhill. The fence has shooting butts built into its course and leads to a crude shelter hut. A drystone wall continues straight downhill to reach **Woldgill Burn**.

If there has been heavy rain and the river is impassable, turn left to follow it downstream. If the water is low, ford the river and climb onto the moorland brow opposite, then turn left to walk down **Woldgill Moss**.

Pass shooting butts and cross a fence, then pass through bracken and ford **Gilderdale Burn**. Turn left to walk downstream on the right-hand bank of Gilderdale Burn.

The way ahead is rugged, but the easiest course is as follows. First, pass through an old gateway in a tumbled drystone wall. Continue downstream until another wall drops steeply to the river, with another old gateway visible. Climb up through the gateway and turn right to climb up through another gateway. Turn left to follow the wall across a moorland slope, looking far ahead to line up other gateways while keeping high above the river. Pass between two small stands of forest, then drift down to Gilderdale Burn to cross a footbridge.

The Pennine Way also crosses the footbridge and can be followed uphill beside a wall. Go past a gateway and climb to join a track, following it further uphill. Pass a couple more gateways while keeping left of the rumpled earthworks of **Whitley Castle**, an old Roman fort.

Head down towards the farm of **Castle Nook**, but step left into a wood and follow a path down to the **A689**. Cross the road to continue along the Pennine Way, along a field path through gates, keeping right of some buildings to go through another gate.

The Pennine Way can be followed back to Slaggyford, but it is easier to use the South Tyne Trail. Drop down to the nearby **Kirkhaugh Station** on the South Tyne Railway. (When trains arrive, refreshments are available from the buffet carriage. Trains can also be used to reach Alston.) Cross a bridge over the line, then pass under the same bridge to follow the trackbed onwards.

Walk past the end of the railway line (but bear in mind that there is a plan to extend it onwards). Cross a bridge over a track at **Kirkhaugh**, then follow the trackbed round a

bend and pass under a bridge. Throughout this stretch, the Pennine Way runs roughly parallel through fields.

An embankment, a cutting and another embankment are passed on the way to **Lintley**, where a farm sits on a knoll. Cross a viaduct here, then pass under a skew arch carrying the **A689**. A soft cutting leads onto an embankment with three bridges beneath it, then the trackbed goes through another cutting, under a bridge, over a bridge, finally reaching a road at **Slaggyford**. Turn right downhill to finish.

The old station site at Slaggyford can be inspected before or after the walk

225

Section 13
THE DALE-HEADS

In an area as bleak and remote as the North Pennines, it's anyone's guess where the true heart of the region lies. The counties of Cumbria, Durham and Northumberland meet on a desolate and boggy moorland crest, marked by a small cairn, above Wearhead, Allenheads and Nenthead. All three dale-heads are blessed with splendid heritage centres telling the story of lead mining in this forbiddingly remote area of the country. Some of the highest roads in England connect these places, and these are among the first to be blocked by snow in the winter, while in high summer the heather is flushed purple.

Four walks explore this central part of the North Pennines AONB. The first walk starts from Allenheads and climbs onto the boggy top of Killhope Law. A broad moorland crest is followed until an easy descent leads quickly back to the village.

Two walks have the lead-mining museum at Killhope in common. One of the walks runs from Cowshill to Killhope along riverside paths, returning over the moors. The other one starts at Killhope and makes a circuit around the very head of Weardale.

The fourth and final walk climbs onto the moors above Nenthead, and stays high for as long as possible before returning to the village through an extensive lead-mining museum. Industrial heritage and extensive moorlands are common themes on these four walks.

The little villages at the dale-heads offer only a small range of facilities, but each one can offer accommodation, food and drink. While there is no public transport from one dale to another, these walking routes have links in common, and can be extended from dale to dale. The dale-head villages also have reasonably good bus services to larger towns down-dale.

WALK 47
Allenheads and Killhope Law

Distance	14km (8¾ miles)
Terrain	A fine moorland track is used at first, followed by rugged walking across bleak moorlands.
Start/finish	Allenheads – 859453
Maps	OS Landranger 87; Explorer OL31
Refreshments	Pub and café at Allenheads.
Transport	Daily Tynedale buses serve Allenheads from Allendale Town and Hexham, except Sundays.

Allenheads is a small village that has completely revitalised itself and boasts a fine heritage centre. A track known as the Carriers Way was once used by packhorses carrying crushed ore from Killhope to the lead-smelting mill at Allenheads. This now provides a fine route to the summit of Killhope Law, and from that point a bleak and boggy moorland crest can be followed around the head of Allendale, with a firm and easy descent at the end.

There are two parallel roads heading down-dale from **Allenheads** – the B6295 and a minor road. Take the latter, which leaves the village and reaches a junction where a left turn is signposted across a bridge at **Slag Hill** for Alston.

Mining trucks outside the Allenheads Inn.

227

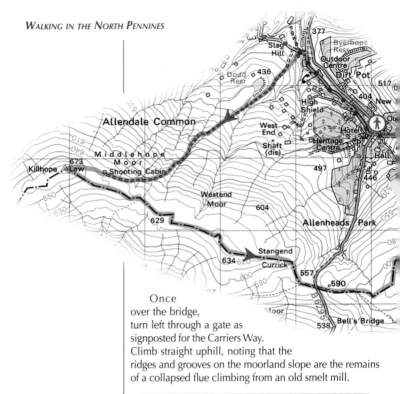

Once over the bridge, turn left through a gate as signposted for the Carriers Way. Climb straight uphill, noting that the ridges and grooves on the moorland slope are the remains of a collapsed flue climbing from an old smelt mill.

CARRIERS WAY

Crushed ore from Killhope was hauled by pack ponies along the Carriers Way, over the moors to Allenheads. The ore was smelted at Slag Hill just outside the village, and sulphurous fumes were conducted up a long, stone-built flue on the moorland slopes of Killhope Law. The flue was periodically swept by young lads to remove condensed substances, ensuring that nothing went to waste.

Either follow the course of the old flue, or take the easier course offered by a stony track that climbs alongside. Sometimes the track has been constructed on top of the ruined flue. Later, a line of grouse-shooting butts is passed, and the track climbs more steeply on **Middlehope Moor**.

There may be a marker post on the left, indicating where the Carriers Way leaves the track and forges straight up to the crest of the moor. However, to climb Killhope Law, stay on the track, which becomes gentle and grassy, to reach a **shooting cabin**.

Walk off the end of the track and follow a rather wet and boggy path onto the broad summit of **Killhope Law**. There is a trig point at 673m (2207ft), a stout cairn and a tall wooden mast, which is something of a landmark and helps identify this otherwise featureless moor in distant views. There are wide-ranging views round the North Pennines in clear weather, but in poor visibility, take care over route-finding when the time comes to leave.

Killhope Law stands on the boundary between Durham and Northumberland, which is marked by a vague groove along the crest of the moorland. Follow this feature, which runs roughly southeast, parallel to the path that was used to reach the summit, and cross the top of the Carriers Way.

Walk straight ahead along the crest of **Westend Moor**, still following the groove through the rugged grass and heather that marks the county boundary. The highest part of the moor rises to 634m (2080ft), then the walking is a bit easier coming down the other side.

When a drystone wall is reached, turn right to follow it, then turn left round a corner and go through a little gate. Follow the wall gently downhill and cross a duckboard over a wet patch. Go through a kissing gate and cross the **B6295**, which exploits a high moorland gap at 587m (1926ft).

Go through a gate on the other side, then follow a path uphill beside a drystone wall. This gives way to a fence that leads onwards to the top of **Burtree Fell**. A

Heather moorlands are crossed before a road is reached at Shorngate Cross

ruined wall joins the fence where a small cairn stands in the heather over 610m (2000ft). Turn left to follow another fence along the heathery crest.

The county boundary is marked by a grassy, boggy groove full of bright-green sphagnum moss, cut straight across a bleak and wet moorland. This is especially boggy when the moor is level. A minor road is reached on a broad gap at **Shorngate Cross**, where a large 'pepperpot' cairn is located.

Turn left to walk along the road, watching for a footpath sign on the left, pointing down a track for Allenheads. The track gives way to a path that crosses a ladder-stile and simply cuts out a sweeping bend to land on the road further downhill. Turn left again to follow the road down to **Allenheads**.

ALLENHEADS

Allenheads was a major centre for the Blackett-Beaumont family's mining concern, known as WB Lead. The family held mining leases for two centuries from 1696. Allenheads Hall was the family's summer residence. In recent decades Allenheads was in serious decline, but it was decided to capitalise on its heritage, and the village is now thriving. Visit the heritage centre, tel 01434 685531, and the Hemmel, the latter being a restaurant in an old byre. The Blacksmith's Shop has exhibits relating to the geology, history and wildlife of the area. An enormous Armstrong hydraulic engine originally provided power for Allenheads, and was eventually brought back 'home' after being moved out of the area. The nearby Allenheads Inn, built in 1770, houses articles from bygone ages, and also provides accommodation, food and drink.

WALK 48
Cowshill and Killhope

Distance	13km (8 miles)
Terrain	Easy riverside paths, a forest, then exposed, high-level moorlands.
Start/finish	Cowshill – 855406
Maps	OS Landranger 87; Explorer OL31
Refreshments	Pub at Cowshill. Café at Killhope.
Transport	Regular daily Weardale buses serve Cowshill from Bishop Auckland and Stanhope, and will occasionally run to Killhope on request.

A fiddly series of riverside paths run from Cowshill to the head of Weardale. There is a splendid lead-mining museum at Killhope, but it takes time to explore properly, and if a visit cannot be made during the walk, then be sure to return some other time to do it justice. A track known as the Carriers Way leads from Killhope onto bleak moorlands. The crest of the moors is all access land, and it can be followed across a high road to Burtree Fell, where a track leads back down to Cowshill.

Start at **Cowshill** by following a minor road downhill to cross **Burtreeford Bridge**. Turn right to start following a path

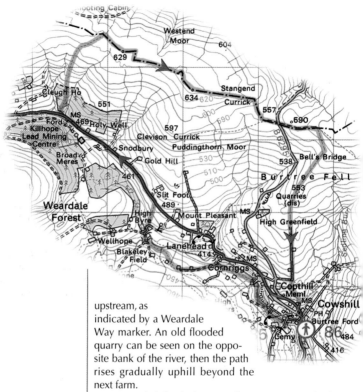

upstream, as indicated by a Weardale Way marker. An old flooded quarry can be seen on the opposite bank of the river, then the path rises gradually uphill beyond the next farm.

Later, drift back down to the river, cross a bridge at **Cornriggs** and follow a path further upstream. When another bridge is reached, don't cross over it, but bear right away from the river to climb up to the A689 road at **Slit Foot**. Turn left to follow the road to **Killhope Wheel** and its lead-mining museum (for details see Walk 49).

To continue the walk, turn right away from the main entrance to the museum and enter a forest. A forest track climbs uphill and emerges in a clear-felled area. Further uphill is a stile over a fence, and beyond it lie open moorland slopes, where the **Carriers Way** is marked by a

sparse line of posts. The path reaches an altitude of 625m (2050ft) and some walkers may wish to detour off to the west to reach the summit of **Killhope Law** (see Walk 47).

To continue with the walk, turn right along the crest of **Westend Moor**. A groove through the rugged grass and heather marks the boundary between Durham and Northumberland. The highest part of the moor rises to 634m (2080ft), then the walking is a bit easier coming down the other side.

When a drystone wall is reached, turn right to follow it, then turn left round a corner and go through a little gate. Follow the wall gently downhill and cross a duckboard over a wet patch. Go through a kissing gate and cross the **B6295**, which exploits a high moorland gap at 587m (1926ft).

Go through a gate on the other side, then follow a path uphill beside a drystone wall. Don't go all the way to the top of **Burtree Fell**, but turn right through a gateway where the wall gives way to a fence. Simply follow the line of a fence downhill, joining a much clearer track that is enclosed in lower pastures. Follow the track down onto the A689 and turn left to return to **Cowshill**.

Fiddly field paths are followed parallel to the River Wear between Cowshill and Killhope

233

WALK 49
Killhope Cross and Knoutberry Hill

Distance	11km (6½ miles)
Terrain	Forest tracks at the start and finish. Mostly exposed, boggy, high-level moorland with some pathless stretches.
Start/finish	Killhope Wheel – 824432
Maps	OS Landranger 86; Explorer OL31
Refreshments	Café at Killhope.
Transport	Regular daily buses serve Cowshill from Bishop Auckland and Stanhope, and will occasionally run to Killhope on request.

Killhope is home to the splendid North of England Lead-Mining Museum, but it takes time to explore properly. This short walk around the head of Weardale should leave at least half a day spare for the task. A track known as the Carriers Way is followed from Killhope towards Killhope Law. The rest of the route runs across access land, and there are some particularly rugged, boggy and pathless stretches, so take care with route-finding in poor visibility. By the time Killhope Cross is reached, navigation is simplified by following fences and walls across the high moors, returning to Killhope along a clear forest track.

KILLHOPE LEAD-MINING MUSEUM

Killhope Wheel is the centrepiece of a remarkable lead-mining centre. The overshot wheel, measuring 10m (33 feet) in diameter, powered machinery inside a crushing mill. Ore came from the Park Level, which can be entered on guided tours. The bousesteads and washing floor have been restored and feature plenty of 'hands-on' exhibits. Buildings have also been restored, and the mine 'shop' is of particular interest. Downstairs is a smithy and stable, while upstairs is a reconstruction of the sleeping quarters, though without the filthy, damp, smelly conditions

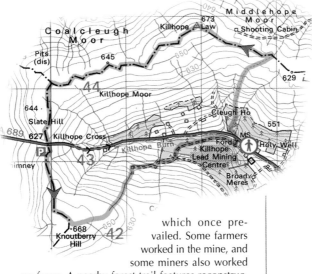

which once pre-vailed. Some farmers worked in the mine, and some miners also worked on farms. A nearby forest trail features reconstructions of typical lead mines throughout the centuries. There is a restaurant on site, as well as a good range of background publications. Tel 01388 537505, www.durham.gov.uk/killhope.

Cross over the road from the main entrance to **Killhope Wheel** and enter a forest. A forest track climbs uphill and emerges in a clear-felled area. Further uphill is a stile over a fence, and beyond it lie open moorland slopes, where the **Carriers Way** is marked by a sparse line of posts.

The path reaches an altitude of 625m (2050ft), where a left turn leads along a groove in the heather, reaching the summit of **Killhope Law**, at 673m (2207ft). A stout cairn, a trig point and a tall wooden mast stand there, offering splendid views around the North Pennines.

Follow the county boundary between Durham and Northumberland, which is a boggy groove along the

235

Walking along the Carrier's Way in the snow on the way to Killhope Law

Killhope Cross sits beside one of the highest roads in England.

moorland crest. It is narrow at first, becoming wider, then is lost in a mess of peat hags, so careful onward navigation is required. A small cairn stands at 648m (2126ft) where the counties of Cumbria, Durham and Northumberland meet, and in a sense this point could claim to be the centre of the North Pennines.

Turn right to trace the remains of the old boundary fence. Very few posts remain upright, but even the fallen ones can be spotted ahead in poor visibility. There is bare peat, heather, crowberry, bilberry and abundant cloudberry.

Head southwards, and a new fence is encountered again at a boundary stone on **Slate Hill**. Walk straight ahead and downhill to a gate onto the main A689 at **Killhope Cross**. This is the highest classified road in England, at 623m (2044ft), and one of the first to be blocked by snow in winter.

Cross the road and go over a step-stile to continue along the moorland crest on the right-hand side of a drystone wall. The line continues with a fence, then a wall again, then another stretch of fence, reaching an area where the peat has been worn down to a stony surface.

A junction of fences is reached just short of **Knoutberry Hill** at 668m (2192ft). Turn left to follow a fence roughly eastwards along a broad moorland crest, reaching a gateway.

Go through the gate and walk down a broad groove on the heather moor, which is used by quad bikes to serve a line of grouse-shooting butts. Continue down to a firm, stony track and follow it through a gate.

Follow the track to a junction with another track beside a forest. Turn left to walk down through the forest, quickly returning to the lead-mining museum car park at **Killhope**.

WALK 50
Nenthead and Nag's Head

Distance	10 or 14km (6¼ or 8¾ miles)
Terrain	Good tracks at the start and finish, but high and boggy moorlands most of the time. Fences and walls make good guides throughout.
Start/finish	Nenthead – 781437
Maps	OS Landrangers 86 and 91; Explorer OL31
Refreshments	Pub, restaurant and café at Nenthead.
Transport	Daily Stagecoach and Wright Brothers buses serve Nenthead from Alston, Brampton and Carlisle, except Sundays. There is also a rare midweek Wright Brothers bus link with Hexham.

The centre of Nenthead stands at 438m (1437ft), and some buildings in the village stand as high as 500m (1640ft). Although it looks haphazard in layout, Nenthead was actually a planned village. It has enjoyed periods of prosperity and neglect, and its old lead mines now form an extensive open-air museum well worth exploring.

This walk climbs from Nenthead onto bleak and barren moors, passing a number of stone curiosities before a descent is made through the Nenthead Mines to return to the village.

A tall cairn stands beside a fence on the summit of Nag's Head above Nenthead.

NENTHEAD

Nenthead looks haphazardly laid out, but was largely a planned settlement whose development was inextricably linked with the nearby lead mines. It is rather quiet today, and facilities are limited to the Miners Arms, Community Shop, Overwater Lodge Restaurant and the Nenthead Mines.

Start at a crossroads in the middle of **Nenthead** and take the road signposted for Greenends. This climbs as a steep, cobbled road to an old school, where a tarmac road continues uphill.

Turn left as the road levels out, then turn right up a clear track signposted as a 'public way' and part of the C2C cycleway. Mountain pansies grow alongside the track, which climbs to a minor road at 609m (1998ft) on **Black Hill**.

Cross over the road and go through a gate onto heather moorland available as access land. Follow a fence gently uphill, and note the remains of an older fence that later veers off to the left. Follow either the new or the old fence, but preferably the old one, which climbs onto the moorland crest to reach a small cairn at 648m (2126ft). This stands where the counties of Cumbria, Durham and Northumberland meet, and in a sense this point could claim to be the centre of the North Pennines.

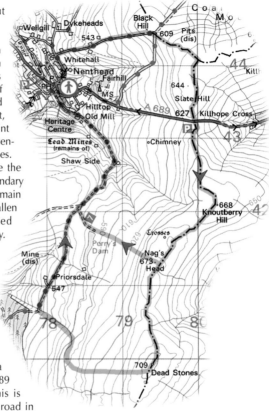

Turn right to trace the remains of the old boundary fence. Very few posts remain upright, but even the fallen ones can be spotted ahead in poor visibility. There is bare peat, heather, crowberry, bilberry and abundant cloudberry.

Head southwards, and the new fence is reached again at a boundary stone on **Slate Hill**. Follow it down to a gate onto the main A689 at **Killhope Cross**. This is the highest classified road in England at 623m (2044ft), and one of the first to be blocked by snow in winter.

Cross the road and go over a step-stile to continue along the moorland crest on the right-hand side of a drystone wall. The line continues with a fence, then a wall again, then another stretch of fence, reaching an area where the peat has been worn down to a stony surface.

A junction of fences is reached just short of **Knoutberry Hill** at 668m (2192ft). Oddly enough, despite

Three little stone crosses can be found by making a detour off-route before Nag's Head

its name, this is one part of the route where cloudberries, or 'knoutberries', are absent.

Keep right to follow a fence roughly southwest, across a broad and gentle boggy dip, to reach another stretch of drystone wall on a moorland hump. At this point, it is worth making a diversion to the right to find the small stone **crosses** marked on the map. These are three in number, and they stand beside a barely discernible ancient track. Head back to the wall and follow another stretch of fencing to the top of **Nag's Head** at 673m (2208ft).

There are two options here: either make an early descent to Perry's Dam and Nenthead, or extend the route to Dead Stones and descend to Priorsdale before returning to Nenthead. In foul weather it is best to descend early, but in fine weather it is well worth the extra effort to extend the route.

To descend early from **Nag's Head,** simply turn right and follow a drystone wall down the moorland slope. This gives way to a stretch of fence, then another wall, then another fence, leading past **Perry's Dam** to join a track. Walk down the track and turn right twice at junctions with broader and clearer tracks in an area of lead-mining spoil.

The track leads down through a valley and straight down through the large open-air attraction of **Nenthead Mines**. Walk all the way to the car park before turning right to return to the middle of **Nenthead**.

To extend the walk from **Nag's Head**, go through a gateway in the drystone wall and keep to the line of the fence, which runs roughly south across a broad and gentle boggy gap.

The fence reaches firmer ground and climbs to a columnar cairn at a junction of fences at 709m (2326ft) on **Dead Stones**. Just below the summit is a drystone hut with a roof and chimney, surrounded by heather, bilberry, crowberry and cloudberry. Views stretch from Cross Fell to Hartside and Cold Fell, all the way round to Weardale, Mickle Fell and nearby Burnhope Seat.

Continue a little south along the fence, then turn right to head east, downhill alongside another fence. This levels out while passing lead-mine spoil, then drops again to a junction of fences. Turn right to follow another fence across the moor, then later it turns left to head downhill beside a crumbling shale ravine.

When a road is reached, turn right to follow it towards the isolated farmstead of **Priorsdale**, but continue straight along a clear track signposted for Nenthead.

The track runs gently up and down, then over a gentle moorland gap to pass close to **Perry's Dam** in an area of lead-mining spoil. The track leads down through a valley and straight down through the large open-air attraction of **Nenthead Mines**. Walk all the way to the car park before turning right to return to the middle of **Nenthead**.

NENTHEAD MINES

A large smelt mill was built by Colonel Liddel in 1738, but he couldn't obtain enough ore for it to be economical. He sold his business to the London Lead Company, or 'Quaker Company', who operated enough mines to keep the mill well supplied.

The benevolence of the company gave Nenthead a couple of 'firsts'. The village was the first place to have compulsory education, and a school was built in 1818 for 200 children. The first free library in the country was built in 1833. The company gained a loyal and well-educated workforce at a time when the North Pennines was the world's largest producer of lead. Robert Bainbridge, an agent for the company, had houses at Nenthead and Middleton-in-Teesdale, and in both places he is commemorated with a cast-iron drinking fountain, though the one at Middleton is more ornate and well kept.

When the Quaker Company ceased mining, operations were continued for a few years by the Vieille Montagne Company. Part of the village centre was cleared to build a five-storey gravity mill that could handle huge quantities of ore, and buildings known as 'the Barracks' housed foreign labourers. Lead mining ceased in 1920, and much of the machinery and buildings have been lost since that time.

Some buildings have been restored in recent years, and the Nenthead Mines are spread across a huge area that takes time to explore. Although the route runs along a right of way through the site, anyone wishing to explore further should note that there is an entry charge, payable at the shop at the main entrance. There is also a café and a bunkhouse on site. Tel 01434 382726, www.npht.com/nentheadmines.

The route finishes by running down through the extensive Nenthead Mines complex

APPENDIX 1

Quick reference guide to routes

1. **Brampton, Gelt and Talkin** *15km (9½ miles)*
   Terrain: gentle field paths, wooded riverside paths and quiet roads
   Start/finish: Moot Hall, Brampton – 531611

2. **Hallbankgate and Cold Fell** *14.5km (9 miles)*
   Terrain: tracks and paths on lower ground, but rugged, boggy
   moorland on higher ground.
   Start/finish: Hallbankgate – 580596

3. **Castle Carrock and Geltsdale** *22km (13½ miles)*
   Terrain: tracks run from valley to valley across moorland slopes,
   followed by paths and minor roads through low-lying fields
   Start/finish: Castle Carrock – 543553

4. **Croglin, Newbiggin and Croglin Fell** *16km (10 miles)*
   Terrain: good firm tracks and paths lead onto and off the moors, but there
   are a couple of river fords and a climb up a rugged moorland slope
   Start/finish: the Robin Hood, Croglin – 574472

5. **Hartside, Black Fell and Renwick** *17.5km (11 miles)*
   Terrain: high moorlands, boggy in places, with few paths. Walls and fences
   can be used as guides. Field paths and tracks are used at a lower level
   Start/finish: Hartside Top Café – 646418

6. **Melmerby and Knapside Hill** *18km (11 miles)*
   Terrain: a good track gives way to broad and open moorland where
   careful navigation is required. Clear tracks are used for the descent
   Start/finish: Melmerby – 616374

7. **Maiden Way – Kirkland to Alston** *19km (12 miles)*
   Terrain: fields give way to open moorland. A ford on the descent can be
   difficult after heavy rain. Good tracks and roads towards the end
   Start: Kirkland – 645325 Finish: Market Cross, Alston – 718465

8. **Blencarn, Cross Fell and Kirkland** *17.5 or 22.5km (11 or 14 miles)*
   Terrain: good tracks and paths on the lower slopes, but rough and boggy
   paths at a higher level, some of which are barely trodden on the ground
   Start/finish: Blencarn – 638312

9.   **Knockergill Pass – Knock to Garrigill** *12 or 22km (7½ or 13½ miles)*
        Terrain: a good track and vague path on the ascent, with a road on the
        highest part. Good tracks and vague paths for the descent, mostly
        beside rivers
        Start: Knock – 680270 or the Fell Road – 715309
        Finish: Dorthgill – 758380 or Garrigill – 745416

10.   **Dufton, Great Rundale and High Cup** *16km (10 miles)*
        Terrain: good tracks from farmland to the high moors, then rugged
        moorland walking, ending with a good path and track
        Start/finish: Dufton – 689250

11.   **Murton, Murton Pike and Murton Fell** *15km (9¼ miles)*
        Terrain: a good track leads onto broad moorlands, but the higher parts
        are pathless and boggy. Good paths and tracks lead down through a
        rugged dale
        Start/finish: Murton – 729220

12.   **Hilton and Tinside Rigg** *18km (11 miles)*
        Terrain: good paths, tracks and roads on lower ground, but rugged and
        sometimes pathless moorland on the higher parts
        Start/finish: Hilton – 735207

13.   **Mickle Fell via the Boundary Route** *12km (7½ miles)*
        Terrain: high-level, exposed, bleak, remote, pathless, rugged moorlands
        Start/finish: Ley Seat, on the B6276 road – 832199

14.   **North Stainmore and Slate Quarry Moss** *13km (8 miles)*
        Terrain: mostly clear tracks and paths on broad, bleak, boggy
        moorlands, but some pathless terrain too
        Start/finish: North Stainmore – 830151

15.   **Kirkby Stephen and Nine Standards** *14km (8¾ miles)*
        Terrain: minor roads, tracks and paths lead up from the fields, but the
        higher moorlands are bleak and boggy
        Start/finish: Kirkby Stephen – 775087

16.   **The Tan Hill and Sleightholme Moor** *14km (9 miles)*
        Terrain: rugged, high-level, exposed moorland paths and tracks
        Start/finish: the Tan Hill Inn – 896067

17.   **Bowes and Bowes Moor** *16km (10 miles)*
        Terrain: easy field paths and farm tracks, with exposed moorland paths
        Start/finish: Bowes – 995135

18. **Greta Bridge and Brignall Banks** *13 or 16km (8 or 10 miles)*
     Terrain: a steep-sided gorge with narrow woodland and field paths
     Start/finish: Greta Bridge – 086133

19. **Barnard Castle and the Tees** *13km (8 miles)*
     Terrain: easy, mostly low-level woodland and riverside paths
     Start/finish: Scar Top, Barnard Castle – 049166

20. **Woodland and Copley** *9km (5½ miles)*
     Terrain: easy, low-level field paths and tracks, with some slopes
     Start/finish: Woodland – 075265

21. **Cotherstone and Romaldkirk** *11km (6½ miles)*
     Terrain: easy, but occasionally rugged riverside paths and field paths
     Start/finish: Fox and Hounds, Cotherstone – 011198

22. **Tees Railway Walk** *11km (6½ miles)*
     Terrain: easy, low-level walking on a railway trackbed
     Start: Middleton-in-Teesdale – 947254
     Finish: Fox and Hounds, Cotherstone – 011198

23. **Middleton and Monk's Moor** *16km (10 miles)*
     Terrain: easy woodland and valley paths, then exposed moorland
     tracks and paths
     Start/finish: Middleton-in-Teesdale – 947254

24. **Middleton and Grassholme** *14km (9 miles)*
     Terrain: fairly good hill paths, then easy low-level paths
     Start/finish: Middleton-in-Teesdale – 947254

25. **Low Force and High Force** *13km (8 miles)*
     Terrain: easy riverside paths, with moorland paths and tracks
     Start/finish: Bowlees Visitor Centre – 907283

26. **Holwick and Hagworm Hill** *24km (15 miles)*
     Terrain: rugged, high-level, bleak and exposed moorlands, sometimes
     with vague paths
     Start/finish: Holwick – 904270

27. **Cronkley Fell** *12km (7½ miles)*
     Terrain: some good tracks, but also exposed moorland paths and a
     rugged riverside path
     Start/finish: Forest-in-Teesdale – 867297

28. **Cow Green and Widdybank Fell** *16km (10 miles)*
     Terrain: easy, though remote roads and good paths
     Start/finish: Cow Green – 810308

29. **Cow Green and Herdship Fell** *16km (10 miles)*
     Terrain: fairly easy moorland tracks and paths, but indistinct towards
     the end
     Start/finish: Cow Green – 810308

30. **Wolsingham and Frosterley** *16km (10 miles)*
     Terrain: mostly easy field paths, moorland tracks and minor roads
     Start/finish: Market Place, Wolsingham – 076373

31. **Stanhope and Stanhope Dene** *8km (5 miles)*
     Terrain: mostly easy field paths and moorland tracks, but occasionally
     pathless with some steep slopes
     Start/finish: Durham Dales Centre, Stanhope – 996392

32. **Westgate, Middlehope and Rookhope** *16km (10 miles)*
     Terrain: easy field paths and tracks, but rough and vague moorland
     paths
     Start/finish: Westgate – 907381

33. **Chapelfell Top and Noon Hill** *11km (7 miles)*
     Terrain: good tracks and paths on the lower slopes, but also rugged,
     exposed, pathless moorland
     Start/finish: St John's Chapel – 885379

34. **Rookhope to Stanhope** *13km (8 miles)*
     Terrain: a high-level moorland track with some steep gradients at the
     start and finish
     Start: Rookhope– 939429
     Finish: Stanhope – 996392

35. **Waskerley Way – Parkhead to Consett** *17km (10½ miles)*
     Terrain: a high-level moorland track giving way to cultivated countryside
     Start: Parkhead Station – 003431
     Finish: Consett – 107508

36. **Edmundbyers and Edmundbyers Common** *14km (9 miles)*
     Terrain: mostly easy tracks and paths up through fields, then back
     across exposed moorlands
     Start/finish: Edmundbyers – 017501

37. **Blanchland and Blanchland Moor** *14km (8¾ miles)*
     Terrain: a fine moorland track leads to a forest, then a more
     difficult moorland path leads to road and gentle riverside walking
     Start/finish: Blanchland – 965503

38. **Devil's Water and Hangman Hill** *10.5km (6½ miles)*
Terrain: fiddly field paths give way to a fine moorland track. A vague
moorland path is followed by a rugged link back to the start
Start/finish: Broadwell House – 911536

39. **Dipton Mill and Dipton Burn** *10km (6 miles)*
Terrain: rugged and well-wooded riverside walking, involving several
fords, along with vague, overgrown or muddy paths
Start/finish: Dipton Mill Inn, near Hexham – 929610

40. **Allen Banks and Staward Gorge** *14km (8¾ miles)*
Terrain: winding riverside paths and narrow paths on steep, wooded slopes
Start/finish: Allen Banks car park – 798640

41. **Allendale Town and Hexhamshire Common** *16km (10 miles)*
Terrain: good tracks and occasional vague paths across broad heather
moorlands, followed by riverside paths and field paths
Start/finish: Allendale Town – 837558

42. **Allendale Town and Allenmill Flues** *12km (7½ miles)*
Terrain: roads, tracks and paths lead to high moorlands, with
roads leading back down into the dale
Start/finish: Allendale Town – 837558

43. **Ninebanks, Hard Rigg and the Dodd** *11 or 20km (7 or 12½ miles)*
Terrain: a good track at the start, then broad and boggy moorland with
walls and fences as guides. Open moorland with vague paths before
the end
Start/finish: Ninebanks Youth Hostel – 771514

44. **Alston, Garrigill and River South Tyne** *14km (8¾ miles)*
Terrain: low-level farm tracks, field paths and occasional roads
Start/finish: Market Cross, Alston – 718465

45. **Alston, Lambley and Haltwhistle** *23km (14¼ miles)*
Terrain: easy, level, firm trackbed through cultivated countryside
and woods
Start: South Tyne Railway, Alston – 717467
Finish: Haltwhistle – 705641

46. **Slaggyford and Grey Nag** *20km (12½ miles)*
    Terrain: a firm track leads onto boggy moorland where fences make useful guides. A rugged descent beside a river links with field paths and an old railway trackbed
    Start/finish: Slaggyford – 677524

47. **Allenheads and Killhope Law** *14km (8¾ miles)*
    Terrain: a fine moorland track is used at first, followed by rugged walking across bleak moorlands
    Start/finish: Allenheads – 859453

48. **Cowshill and Killhope** *13km (8 miles)*
    Terrain: easy riverside paths, a forest, then exposed, high-level moorlands
    Start/finish: Cowshill – 855406

49. **Killhope Cross and Knoutberry Hill** *11km (6½ miles)*
    Terrain: forest tracks at the start and finish. Mostly exposed, boggy, high-level moorland with some pathless stretches
    Start/finish: Killhope Wheel – 824432

50. **Nenthead and Nag's Head** *10 or 14km (6¼ or 8¾ miles)*
    Terrain: good tracks at the start and finish, but high and boggy moorlands most of the time. Fences and walls make good guides throughout
    Start/finish: Nenthead – 781437

APPENDIX 2
North Pennines Administration Contacts

The North Pennines Area of Outstanding Natural Beauty is covered by three county councils. The eastern parts of Cumbria, the western parts of County Durham, and the southern parts of Northumberland meet in the heart of the North Pennines. The county councils employ countryside staff and have a responsibility for the upkeep of rights of way. Any problems with rights of way or access land can be reported to the relevant council. The North Pennines AONB Partnership works with several statutory and voluntary organisations to look after the North Pennines, conserve and enhance its natural beauty and heritage, and improve local services.

North Pennines AONB
North Pennines AONB Partnership, Weardale Business Centre, The Old Co-op Building, 1 Martin Street, Stanhope, Co Durham, DL13 2UY. Tel 01388 528801, www.northpennines.org.uk.

Cumbria County Council
Cumbria County Council, The Courts, Carlisle, Cumbria, CA3 8NA. Tel 01228 606060, www.cumbria.gov.uk.

Durham County Council
Durham County Council, County Hall, Durham, DH1 5UL. Tel 0191 3834567, www.durham.gov.uk.

Northumberland County Council
Northumberland County Council, County Hall, Morpeth, Northumberland, NE61 2EF. Tel 01670 533000, www.northumberland.gov.uk.

APPENDIX 3
Public Transport

The last time a reasonably comprehensive brochure was produced listing most of the public transport around the North Pennines was in 2007. There seem to be no plans to reintroduce such a publication, which leaves readers the awkward task of tracking down individual timetable leaflets. Throughout this guidebook, the names of local operators are given so that contact can be made with them. The vast majority of routes in this guidebook were researched using local bus services.

Airports
Newcastle Airport, tel 0871 8821121, www.newcastleairport.com
Tees Valley Airport, tel 0871 2242426, www.durhamteesvalleyairport.com
Leeds Bradford International Airport, www.lbia.co.uk

Newcastle Ferryport
DFDS Seaways, tel 0871 5229955, www.dfdsseaways.co.uk

Trains
Cross Country trains, tel 0844 8110124, www.crosscountrytrains.co.uk
National Express East Coast, www.nationalexpresseastcoast.com
Northern Rail, www.northernrail.org
Weardale Railway, www.weardale-railway.org.uk
South Tyne Railway, www.strps.org.uk

Buses
National Express, tel 0871 7818181, www.nationalexpress.com
Arriva, tel 0870 1201088, www.arrivabus.co.uk
Stagecoach, www.stagecoachbus.com
Classic Coaches, www.classic-coaches.co.uk
Fellrunner, tel 01768 88232, www.fellrunnerbus.co.uk
Robinson's, Appleby, contact Traveline
Grand Prix, tel 017683 41328, www.grandprixservices.co.uk
Hodgson's, tel 01833 630730
Upper Teesdale bus, tel 01833 640213
Weardale Motor Services, tel 01388 528235, www.weardalemotorservices.co.uk
Go-North East, tel 0845 6060260, www.simplygo.com
Tynedale, tel 01434 322944
Wright Brothers, tel 01434 381200

Traveline
Timetable information can be checked for any form of public transport in or around the North Pennines by contacting Traveline, tel 0871 2002233, www.traveline.org.uk

APPENDIX 4
Tourist Information and Visitor Centres

Tourist Information Centres
Alston, tel 01434 382244, www.visiteden.co.uk
Appleby, tel 017683 51177, www.applebytown.org.uk
Barnard Castle, tel 01833 690909, www.visitteesdale.com
Bishop Auckland, tel 01388 604922, www.bishopaucklandtownhall.org.uk
Brampton, tel 01697 73433, www.historic-carlisle.org.uk
Corbridge, tel 01434 632815, www.hadrianswallcountry.org
Haltwhistle, tel 01434 322002, www.hadrianswallcountry.org
Hexham, tel 01434 652220, www.hadrianswallcountry.org
Kirkby Stephen, tel 017683 71199, www.visiteden.co.uk
Middleton-in-Teesdale, tel 01833 641001, www.middletonplus.org.uk
Penrith, tel 01768 867466, www.visiteden.co.uk
Stanhope, tel 01388 527650, www.durhamdalescentre.co.uk

Visitor Centres
Allendale Heritage Centre, tel 01434 685531
Bowlees Visitor Centre, tel 01833 622292
Durham Dales Centre, Stanhope, tel 01388 527650, www.durhamdalescentre.co.uk
Harehope Quarry, Frosterley, tel 01388 528599, www.harehopequarry.org
Killhope – The North of England Lead Mining Museum, tel 01388 537505,
www.durham.gov.uk/killhope
Nenthead Mines Heritage Centre, tel 01434 382726,
www.npht.com/nentheadmines
RSPB Geltsdale, tel 01697 746717, www.rspb.org.uk
South Tyne Railway, Alston, tel 01434 381696, www.strps.co.uk
Upper Teesdale and Moor House national nature reserves, tel 01833 622374
Weardale Museum of High House Chapel, tel 01388 517433,
www.weardalemuseum.co.uk
Weardale Railway, tel 0845 6001348, www.weardale-railway.org.uk

LISTING OF CICERONE GUIDES

For full and up-to-date information
on our ever-expanding list of guides,
please visit our website:
www.cicerone.co.uk.

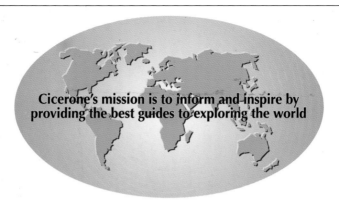

Cicerone's mission is to inform and inspire by providing the best guides to exploring the world

Since its foundation 40 years ago, Cicerone has specialised in publishing guidebooks and has built a reputation for quality and reliability. It now publishes nearly 300 guides to the major destinations for outdoor enthusiasts, including Europe, UK and the rest of the world.

Written by leading and committed specialists, Cicerone guides are recognised as the most authoritative. They are full of information, maps and illustrations so that the user can plan and complete a successful and safe trip or expedition – be it a long face climb, a walk over Lakeland fells, an alpine cycling tour, a Himalayan trek or a ramble in the countryside.

With a thorough introduction to assist planning, clear diagrams, maps and colour photographs to illustrate the terrain and route, and accurate and detailed text, Cicerone guides are designed for ease of use and access to the information.

If the facts on the ground change, or there is any aspect of a guide that you think we can improve, we are always delighted to hear from you.

Cicerone Press
2 Police Square Milnthorpe Cumbria LA7 7PY
Tel: 015395 62069 Fax: 015395 63417
info@cicerone.co.uk www.cicerone.co.uk

CICERONE